Photo by Sharon Risedorph

Canopy, 60″ × 56″ (150cm × 140cm), Gloria Loughman

Luminous Landscapes

QUILTED VISIONS IN PAINT & THREAD

Gloria Loughman

C&T PUBLISHING

Text and artwork © 2007 Gloria Loughman

Artwork © 2007 C&T Publishing, Inc.

Publisher: **Amy Marson**

Editorial Director: **Gailen Runge**

Acquisitions Editor: **Jan Grigsby**

Editor: **Lynn Koolish**

Technical Editors: **Helen Frost, Robyn Gronning**

Copyeditor/Proofreader: **Wordfirm Inc.**

Cover Designer: **Kristen Yenche**

Design Director/Book Designer: **Rose Sheifer-Wright**

Illustrator: **John Heisch**

Production Assistant: **Tim Manibusan**

Photography: **Tony Loughman**, unless otherwise noted

Library of Congress Cataloging-in-Publication Data

Loughman, Gloria.
  Luminous landscapes : quilted visions in paint and thread / Gloria Loughman.
    p. cm.
  ISBN-13: 978-1-57120-366-3 (paper trade : alk. paper)
  ISBN-10: 1-57120-366-4 (paper trade : alk. paper)
  1. Machine quilting. 2. Patchwork. I. Title.

TT835.L69 2007
746.46'041--dc22

                                    2006016299

Printed in China
10 9 8 7 6 5 4 3

Dedication

I would like to dedicate this book to my husband, Tony; our three daughters, Amanda, Sarah, and Rebecca; and my parents, Florence and Jack Jeffery.

Acknowledgments

To my husband, Tony: What a partnership we shared as we worked together on this project. There should be two names on the cover. Thank you for the countless hours you spent taking wonderful photographs. Your patience, understanding, support, and love made the many long days spent working on this book together another highlight of the thirty-six years we have shared.

To our three daughters, Amanda, Sarah, and Rebecca: You are all successful professional women in your own fields. Your enthusiasm, whole-hearted support, advice, and practical assistance were invaluable and much appreciated.

To my students: You generously allowed me to showcase your beautiful quilts in this book. Thank you for sharing your work so that others may be inspired and feel empowered to tackle their own designs.

To the members of the Kerang Quilters: Thank you for your fellowship and friendship over the past fifteen years. Your encouragement and support for me as a teacher gave me confidence to extend my horizons and pursue my dreams.

To my editor, Lynn Koolish: Thank you for your thoughtful and constructive comments over the time spent writing this book. Your understanding of a busy teacher's hectic schedule, your empathy for a novice author, and your enthusiasm and encouragement ensured that this process was a fulfilling and enjoyable experience for me.

To my technical editor, Helen Frost: Your thoughtful comments, your efforts to make sure each detail was accurate, and your insight and positive observations were much appreciated.

Finally, thank you to the whole team at C&T. It has been a wonderful experience working with such a highly regarded and very amenable company.

contents

Bingil Bay, 72″ × 90″ (180cm × 225cm), Gloria Loughman

introduction

Life is full of surprises...

Life is full of surprises. It can throw you challenges and take you on marvelous adventures.

As a young child growing up in the rural outskirts of Melbourne, I spent most of my waking hours outdoors, climbing trees, collecting eggs on my grandparents' poultry farm, and even minding snakes while my grandfather searched for big sticks to kill them.

As a teenager, I loved sports and was a member of every sporting club in our neighborhood. At that time in my life, sewing was certainly a challenge, and, indeed, I managed to fail needlework at school. I initially trained to be a teacher of physical education and mathematics, and later on completed further study to become a special education teacher.

My husband, Tony, believes that he made his biggest mistake more than thirty years ago, in 1974, when he bought me the latest top-of-the-line Bernina sewing machine for Christmas. Mastering dressmaking was certainly a challenge, but with three daughters, I put that wonderful machine through its paces.

In 1988, still in my thirties, I was diagnosed with breast cancer. Toward the end of my treatment, a friend invited me to a patchwork class. In my fragile state, still recovering from the debilitating effects of chemotherapy, I planned to create a family heirloom, perhaps something to leave behind for my young daughters. However, I discovered early on that I wasn't meant to be a hand quilter, so that first quilt was never actually finished. Luckily, I have had many more years to make some special quilts.

I have a close affinity with the Australian bush— I love all its moods and amazing changes of color.

Having had the opportunity to travel to many unique and fascinating parts of our continent, I am continually challenged to reproduce images of the bush in thread and paint. As a textile artist, I believe we see things of beauty that others just pass by. How lucky we are to have such a wonderful life.

Now the adventure really begins. The opportunities to travel and teach in so many places have been unbelievable. With family in Switzerland, I have readily accepted any invitation to teach in Europe. I have also enjoyed the hospitality of the New Zealand Quilters on many occasions and have come to admire their skills and wonderful use of color. Visits to teach in the United States and Japan have also widened my horizons as I have met with so many dedicated teachers and students. In Australia, my favorite classes are often in the small country towns, where students approach the classes with unlimited energy and ideas. Their delight at creating an original design is infectious, and I am rewarded time and time again by their growing confidence and enthusiasm.

This book is a result of repeated requests from my students to write it all down. They believed I could do it and that I had something worthwhile to share. I am forever grateful for their enthusiasm and endeavors, and I am proud to include some of their work in the gallery section.

Having worked as a special education teacher for fifteen years, I know that we all have different abilities, talents, and skills. I have endeavored to make the information in this book easy to understand but still informative and detailed for those who enjoy the challenge of creating their own designs.

Photo by Sharon Risedorph

Kimberley Mystique, 80″ × 88″ (200cm × 220cm), Gloria Loughman

Have you yearned to make a landscape quilt that captures your memories of a special place? It might be a holiday destination, a special place from your childhood, or even the view from your kitchen window. Where do you start? What are the key steps to making your landscape an achievable project?

The process of creating a beautiful landscape quilt requires decisions about design and color, as well as accurate construction techniques and embellishing. This chapter will focus on the design component; the other elements will be addressed in later chapters.

Boab tree, coast of Western Australia   Cluster of boab trees

We all see the world around us in different ways. Even when we look at the same scene, we see it differently. Previous experiences, differences in how we physically perceive color, and our personal taste influence the way we view a scene. When you make a landscape quilt, you should try to capture not the actual landscape, but your personal perception of the scene. You may decide on true-to-life details or a more abstract form. Thus, a wonderful variety of interpretations of landscapes are possible.

Inspiration

When considering the inspiration for your design, look for something that interests and excites you visually. It doesn't have to be an idyllic vista or rolling hills and sparkling streams. Many stunning landscapes have been produced from quite unlikely sources.

Creating in a vacuum is difficult, so surround yourself with resources. Inspiration can come from cookbooks, gardening books, calendars, holiday brochures, art magazines, postcards, nature books, and personal photographs. Check out your local library and even surf the Internet. Collecting resources is one of my favorite parts of the design process.

My quilt *Kimberley Mystique* (opposite page) was based on the boab trees that grow in the rugged terrain in far northwest Australia. The sight of these seemingly magical trees rewarded my long, and at times arduous, trip to this remote part of Australia. I photographed the trees at different times of the day, sketched them, collected pictures of them, camped next to them, and on occasion even hugged a few. In the evenings, and occasionally the early mornings, I gazed at the beautiful sunset and sunrise skies. After gradually collecting my resources, I was ready to start the design process.

My first step was to sketch my design, and in reality I would do at least fifty sketches, or more, until I was happy with the result.

One of the sunset photos became the inspiration for my sky. A number of different trees from various locations seemed to work well together and became the star players. I was keen to include an area of water in my quilt because the water could reflect the light from the sunset, but how could I incorporate this in the arid northwest? The answer was quite simple, although at first not obvious. The scene had to be in summer, which is the wet season when the land is flooded.

So I had my key elements—the sunset sky, my wonderfully shaped trees, and the flooded plains reflecting the sky colors. Now how to put all these elements together?

Ayers Rock, Uluru

Sky colors reflected in water
Sky colors reflected in water
Trees unite sky with foreground.

Composition

Composition is the basic structure of a scene, and we can liken composition to our skeletons or to the framework of a building. Planning, especially if you are making a large quilt, helps you avoid ending up in a muddle after weeks or even months of work.

Now this is your quilt, so you can do what you like. Some artists strive to make their landscapes look as much like the original scene as possible. Others, like me, play with the elements and use the photos only as a starting point.

Harmony

When considering composition, the main thing you need to achieve is a feeling of harmony and balance, a feeling of unity, where shapes, colors, tones, and all the elements of the composition are in sync with each other.

Linking and Overlapping

You can create harmony by placing some elements close together, by overlapping elements, or by some other continuous arrangement. Some landscapes need lines that connect different areas. In this way, a tree or a building can unite the sky with the bottom of the picture.

Color

When creating a landscape, it is the sky that sets the tone for the rest of the color decisions. If you have a body of water in your design, remember that the water reflects the sky color. If the sky is blue, then usually the water will look more natural if it is blue as well. Shades of violet in the sky look effective when carried through to hints of violet in the sea, the foliage, or the land itself. Reducing the number of colors can also assist you in the quest for harmony. (For a detailed discussion of using color to create harmony, see page 18.)

Sunset at Port Augusta

Beautiful sunset sky

Repetition

When making a landscape quilt, you are also making decisions about the shapes of the fabric pieces you are stitching together to create the work. Repetition of shapes can provide cohesion, even if the sizes and colors of the pieces are different. The multicolored sunset sky in *Kimberley Mystique* (page 6) is made up of diamonds cut from many different fabrics and stitched together. To create a feeling of synergy, I replicated these diamond shapes in the trunks of the trees in a few places. The size, the color, the texture, and even the alignment are different, but a definite link between the sky and trees has been created.

Diamond shapes are featured in sky.

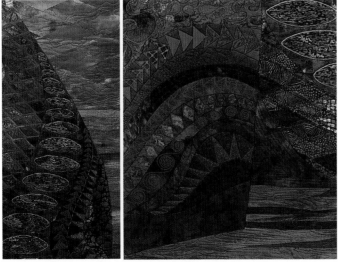

Diamond shapes are repeated in many areas to create harmony.

Visual Movement

When you arrange shapes for your quilt, take inspiration from nature, which is full of directional movement. Vertical and horizontal lines are usually man-made; it is the more natural diagonal lines that are vital to bring energy and movement to your design.

Diagonal lines provide movement and energy.

Directional Lines

Try sketching your design as a series of directional lines. Can you feel that sense of movement? Perhaps changing the direction of some of the elements or changing the angles between the elements will help achieve the movement you want.

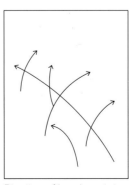

Directions of key elements in **Grass Trees** (page 15)

Take advantage of lines that lead the eye into the design, and leave out elements that lead to the outer edge and out of the quilt. Ideally, once the eye has been led into a work, it should be held inside for as long as possible. Sometimes you can create a sense of flow that meanders around the work, taking the eye on a journey through the main features. These flow lines can be created using the edge of a building, the top of a hill, or the curve of a tree limb. Avoid adding something bold and distracting on the edge of the quilt because it will usually detract from the composition, causing the eye to dart to the side of the work.

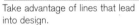

Take advantage of lines that lead into design.

Outside foliage creates flow lines that lead around work.

Create Areas of Space

Space in a design is necessary to give the eye room to travel around and then rest before being led back to the most interesting part, the focal point. If the design is overcrowded and fussy, the eye will be led along too many paths in the search for something satisfying and eventually may give up altogether if the process is too demanding.

Always be aware of the negative spaces between the shapes you have made. Give breathing space to the busier areas of textures and patterns by not allowing unnecessary lines and shapes to crowd in wherever a space exists.

Framing Your Subject

Placing a frame in the foreground leads the eye into the picture. This technique helps give viewers a sense of where they are standing to observe the scene. The frame could be an archway, shutters on a window, the branches of a tree, a curtain of fine leaves, or perhaps elements spilling out into the borders. The frame directs attention toward the focal point (see next page) and creates an interesting composition. The frame can be a natural or man-made element, and it often covers at least two edges. It needs to have some interesting characteristic of its own, be it shape, texture, or color. It must not detract from the main focus but direct attention toward the main subject. In an evening scene, the frame could be a silhouette, creating a stunning result.

Interesting shapes and angles created by man-made framing.

Twilight scene is framed by glowing tree.

Balance and Focal Point

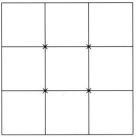

Rule of thirds: suggested points for placement of focal point

We've already mentioned "focal point," but what is it and where should you place it? The focal point is the feature that draws your eye first. Often the focal point stands out because of its high contrast with surrounding areas. Students of graphic design and photography learn to place the focal point off center and then balance this weight with other elements in the picture. The commonly used "rule of thirds" is based on the theory that the eye goes naturally to a point about two-thirds of the way up a page.

Asymmetric balance, or informal balance, is generally considered more pleasing than symmetric balance. Placing the focal point off center and balancing its weight with other objects will be much more effective than placing the main feature dead center. Balance in a design is similar to balance in the physical sense. Put too much weight on one side and your design is in danger of tipping over; viewers will find it uncomfortable and a little disturbing to look at.

Balanced, but not visually exciting

Improved visually, but weight on one side is obviously unbalanced.

Adding smaller tree improves balance.

Smaller tree moved further into background gives better feel of balance and is pleasing visually.

Lines of trunk lead to focal point.

Rocky outcrop is positioned off center.

Sunset Safari, 25″ × 19″ (64cm × 48cm), Gloria Loughman
Lower horizon to show off a sky.

Tropical Seascape, 28″ × 22″ (70cm × 56cm), Gloria Loughman
When area of interest is land or water, leave just small section of sky.

Try to overcome the natural tendency to cut your work in half by placing the horizon across the center. If the area of interest is land or water, the horizon should usually be about two-thirds of the way up from the lower edge. On the other hand, if you want to showcase your beautifully painted sunset sky, lower the horizon line to approximately one-third of the way up from the bottom.

Contrast

In addition to creating harmony, you must also consider your design in terms of contrast. If a scene is entirely light, it can look washed out, and the design can be indiscernible. On the other hand, a design that uses all dark colors can look somber and dull. When I visit a gallery, paintings or quilts that have a strong impact on me are those in which the artist has used light effectively. Sometimes the placement of a touch of light produces a powerful effect on a dark background, and the brilliance of a clear color contrasting against a murky background can be breathtaking.

Light

When you are planning a design, the light source is a critical factor. The light determines the range and intensity of your colors, the placement and depth of the shadows, and the overall atmosphere of your work.

You will need to vary the value of the colors in the landscape so the viewer can easily distinguish between the elements. Record the direction of your light source to assist you when creating shadows and areas of strong contrast, keeping in mind that you must also ensure that the contrasts are not too harsh and overwhelming.

Note light source.

Shadows indicate direction of light source.

When considering contrast, pose the question, "Does my focal point demand enough attention?" Subduing colors and textures around the focal point can certainly direct the eye to this feature.

Complementary Colors

As well as considering contrast in terms of light and dark, you should consider other contrasts to make your work more dynamic. Complementary colors can enliven areas of low contrast. Complementary colors, which are opposite each other on the color wheel (for example, yellow and purple, or orange and blue), appear particularly vibrant when placed next to each other. A mere touch can be enough—don't overdo it! (See more on color starting on page 15.)

The adjacent red and green appear vibrant.

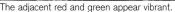
Overlapping grasses and trees give feeling of depth.

Further Contrasts

When you are looking for something to make your work more exciting and appealing, other contrasts to consider are those be-tween large and small objects, cold and warm colors, textured and plain surfaces. (For detailed information and advice on creating contrast with color, see pages 19–20.)

Creating Perspective

Another critical design element you need to consider is perspective, or depth. There are a number of techniques you can use to create this illusion.

One way to develop a feel for perspective is to copy or trace the lines of a photograph, translating it into the language of lines. I prefer freehand sketching to tracing, but I recommend the latter to begin with because you can trace in a few accurate lines that you can build on. Learn to see perspective wherever you are. Through your new perspective eye, you can concentrate on the lines and not be distracted by other elements.

Photographs of potential subjects often reveal fences and roads that you may not have noticed when you took the picture. If these lines are horizontal, and cut across the foreground, they can be distracting and obstruct an easy entry for the eye. However, an empty foreground that provides nothing to help the eye enter the scene can negate a feeling of perspective.

Overlapping Objects

Using overlapping objects in the foreground to hide or partially obscure objects in the middle distance or objects directly behind the foreground goes a long way toward creating depth. The suggestion that one object is behind another forces your mind to perceive a feeling of space.

Objects in the Distance

Placing large and small versions of similar objects in a design can also suggest space and depth.

Flowers appear smaller in distance.

Large and small trees suggest depth.

Textured fabrics stand out.

Textured patterns in sand fade as they move into background.

Leaves gradually lose clarity as they move into the background.

Another point to remember is that the amount of detail you can see depends on how close you are to an object. Objects lose detail and clarity as they are placed further back in a composition. For the background, choose fabrics with blurred and indistinct patterns, in contrast to the foreground, which demands fabrics with more detail and texture.

To illustrate this point, consider a fabric with small pine trees. The scale of the trees is quite suitable for distant mountains covered in pine trees. But when this fabric is used in the background of a quilt, the distinct pattern of the foliage makes the fabric jump forward in the design. A hand-dyed or similar tone-on-tone fabric that reads as a pine forest because of its appropriate color would be a better choice.

Converging Lines

When considering design features such as roads, rivers, and buildings, remember that the lines made by these features appear to converge as they move away from you.

Perspective usually starts in the foreground and leads into the composition.

Aerial Perspective

Put simply, aerial perspective is the effect of distance and atmosphere on color. Colors become duller and lighter as they recede into the distance. In addition, the impurities in the atmosphere tinge elements with blue or gray as they recede. So careful selection of colors can also help in creating the illusion of depth. (There is a lot more information on creating perspective with color starting on page 21.)

Building lines converge toward background.

Rows of tulip fields converge toward horizon.

color is magic

Color is magic! Color is exciting! It is probably the most powerful element of quiltmaking. Color can stir a variety of emotions. For some people, color sense comes naturally and is instinctive. But many of us have to learn to use color effectively through study and experience. Finding the magic is much easier if you understand the basics.

Grass Trees, 47″ × 71″ (120cm × 180cm), Gloria Loughman

Photo by Sharon Risedorph

Selecting Your Color Scheme

Once you have settled on the design of your quilt, it is time to think about color. Should you copy the scene exactly, rendering the colors and tones as you see them? Perhaps you could try to improve what you see using a little imagination, bringing in other colors to complement what is already before you. It is possible to change the colors without losing the integrity of a scene. You can adjust the colors of the background, intensify the colors of the vegetation, or perhaps even transform the whole scene by replacing the blue sky in the photograph with a stunning sunset.

Don't limit yourself when it comes to color. There is an immense range of beautiful colors just waiting for you. But working with too many colors in one quilt can be a disaster. You can end up with a quilt that has little harmony or balance and is oddly disturbing to the eye. Try practicing with a limited palette and see how many effects you can create with two or three colors. But where to start? Which colors go together?

The best way to begin is by learning to use color schemes—combinations of colors based on logical relationships between colors around the color wheel. Using these color schemes ensures that your work will have cohesive, eye-catching colors, and helps minimize color mistakes while still allowing for delightful surprises.

The Color Wheel

The color wheel is made up of colors arranged around and inside a circle. All the colors on the outside of the circle are pure, bright colors, and those on the inside are lighter, duller, or darker colors.

Primary Colors

The primary colors are pure and have no other color in them. These colors are equidistant from one another on the color wheel and are the foundation for mixing all other colors.

Secondary Colors

Secondary colors are mixed from the primaries and are located midway on the color wheel.

Tertiary Colors

Tertiary colors are located between the primary and secondary colors and are mixtures of the two.

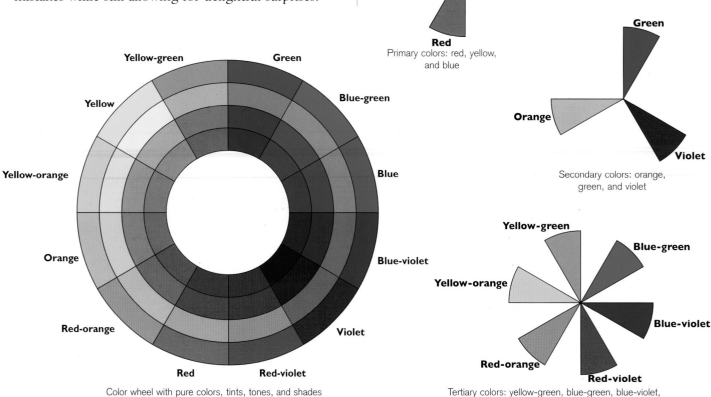

Primary colors: red, yellow, and blue

Secondary colors: orange, green, and violet

Tertiary colors: yellow-green, blue-green, blue-violet, red-violet, red-orange, and yellow-orange

Color wheel with pure colors, tints, tones, and shades

Hue

Hue describes a color itself and is the quality or characteristic by which we can distinguish one color from another. It is the name of the color.

Value

Value is the relative lightness or darkness of a color. Value creates mood and atmosphere. A group of dark colors that are similar in value will reflect a somber, mysterious mood, whereas a contrasting range that includes many lights and darks will result in a vibrant, high-energy ambience. Pink and maroon, for example, are in the red family, but they differ in value. You can add white or black to a color to change its value.

Tints

Tints are the softer, more delicate colors. They are created by adding white to a color. They can be used to create a feeling of peace and tranquility. Although not vibrant, they can be beautiful and are often seen at sunrise.

Tones (Color Intensity)

Color intensity, or chroma, is the brightness or dullness of a color. Create tones by diluting the pure colors on the outside of the color wheel with grays. Other wonderful tones can be created by mixing colors that are opposite each other on the color wheel.

Nature provides many examples of tones. They can be beautiful, peaceful, and calming like the colors of fallen leaves or pebbles lining a riverbed. Consider the myriad tones in a sunset sky, and the range of blues in our oceans.

Shades

Shades are created by adding varying amounts of black to a color. Add black to warm colors for autumn shades such as rust, olive-green, and brown. Add black to cool colors for evening colors and dark, mysterious woodland colors such as deep teals, indigos, navy blues, and dark greens.

Tulip field in analogous colors   Purple petals with contrasting yellow center   Canola fields against blue-violet sky

Color Schemes

Planning Color Schemes

The temptation to create what you see rather than what you feel can mostly be overcome by planning a color scheme before you actually start painting or selecting fabric. Interestingly, the more you know about color and the better you understand structured color schemes, the more individual and personal your color choices become. Your work becomes richer and more powerful. Here are some ways to create your own color palette:

■ Clip color schemes that you like from magazines. Pin them to a bulletin board in your studio and refer to them often for inspiration.

■ Use a natural object as inspiration for your color schemes. Mother Nature is never wrong.

■ Create color palettes in a visual diary that will become a ready reference, always available and ready to use.

■ Start with a limited number of hues in your work. More colors can be created by intermixing the original colors and by altering value or chroma levels.

■ Read books on color and observe how other artists use it.

■ Select a favorite artist's work and analyze his or her color choices.

■ Relax and enjoy color. Most artists will admit that although color can be challenging and at times even frustrating, it can also give fulfillment and satisfaction.

Monochromatic Color Scheme

A monochromatic color scheme (one color) is the simplest and is based on color similarity. A monochromatic color scheme can be lightened or darkened in value by adding white or black to the colors, or dulled in intensity by adding gray.

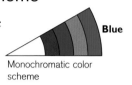
Monochromatic color scheme

Value is the most important aspect of this color scheme. The areas with the strongest contrast will attract the eye, and as the colors fade off in the distance, they will create perspective. Squint your eyes at your original, or make a black-and-white photocopy of it—this will allow you to see the values rather than the color.

Color in a sketch of your design in shades of a single color to ensure that the perspective is working, and that you have sufficient contrast to highlight your focal point before attempting to make the design in fabric. Keep in mind that getting enough fabrics of only one color in the required range of values is a challenge, unless you dye or paint them yourself.

Analogous Color Scheme

Another scheme based on similarity is the analogous color scheme. It is considered to be one of the most beautiful schemes to work with because you are using adjacent colors on the wheel. You can use up to five colors. Many exquisite colorings in nature superbly illustrate this harmony.

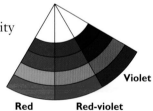
Analogous color scheme

Quilt made in just one color   Quilt made in analogous colors   Quilt in complementary red and green color scheme

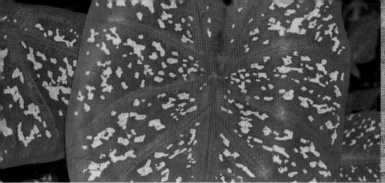

Stunning red-violet and yellow-green leaves

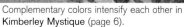

Complementary colors intensify each other in
Kimberley Mystique (page 6).

Complementary Color Scheme

Complementary color schemes are based on differences rather than similarities. Complementary colors are directly opposite each other on the color wheel. Thus blue/orange and yellow-green/red-violet are two of the many complementary color schemes. To create work that has wonderful color balance and is visually pleasing, follow the advice commonly given to artists: Put a little bit of warm color in the cool color, or put a little bit of cool color in the warm. We often see complementary color schemes in nature. Sometimes the scheme is dramatic and exciting, and at other times it is subtle and can almost be overlooked.

Complementary colors are beautiful when a variety of tints and shades are used. Try mixing varying amounts of the two colors together. The resulting colors will work well together because all the mixed colors have hints of the two original colors. Using such a palette creates a strong and pleasing composition.

When placed next to each other, complementary pairs will intensify each other's chroma to create drama and impact. For example, when blue is placed beside orange, the blue will look more intensely blue and the orange more intensely orange.

When using a complementary color scheme, be sure that one color is dominant. If both colors have equal visual power, they will compete visually, and the design will suffer. The viewer's eyes will jump from one spot to another, not knowing where to rest. Relate the dominant color to the chosen subject. For example rusty boats, glowing rocks, or a sunset sky would suit a dominant warm (orange) scheme, with the blue complements in the background. For something with an emphasis on water or a midday sky, make the cool blues dominant, supported by toned-down warm oranges.

Scene with dominant cool water

Scene with dominant warm rocks

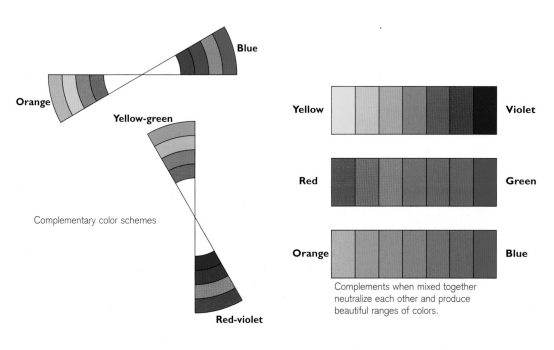

Blue

Orange

Yellow-green

Complementary color schemes

Red-violet

Yellow						Violet

Red						Green

Orange						Blue

Complements when mixed together neutralize each other and produce beautiful ranges of colors.

Split Complementary Color Scheme

For a split complementary color scheme, begin by choosing three analogous colors to convey the dominant mood of the design. Then take the middle color and select its complement. In your design, make the analogous colors dominant, varying value and intensity. Use the complement for color accents.

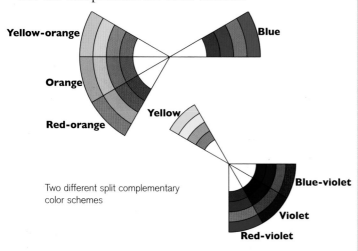

Two different split complementary color schemes

This is my favorite color scheme. I love the dramatic impact and excitement that the accent color brings to a quilt. It is harmonious and rich, yet it still has contrast and strength. (See *Kimberley Mystique,* page 6, and *Grass Trees,* page 15).

In addition to using the four pure colors, use their tints and shades. To make your composition even more exciting, you can use the neutralized colors that result from mixing the hues with their complements.

Double Complementary Color Scheme

Try using two adjacent colors, or choose two colors that are separated from each other by another color on the wheel and then add their complements. These combinations provide brilliant contrasts and exciting color.

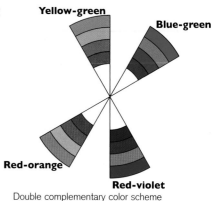

Double complementary color scheme

Triadic Color Scheme

The basis of the triadic color scheme is the relationship between colors that are equidistant from each other on the color wheel. The success of this scheme usually depends on giving a major role to one color family. One of the other families becomes the secondary player, with the third having a minor role.

Triadic color scheme

To find triadic color schemes, select your feature color then find the other colors that are four steps away—for example, violet, orange, and green.

Remember that you can also use tints and shades of the colors, as well as mixing the colors together.

Quilt in split complementary color scheme

Quilt in triadic color scheme

Triadic color scheme of striking yellow and red flowers against blue backdrop

On clear days, mountains become lighter and bluer as they move into distance.

On overcast days, mountains become paler and grayer.

Sky is lighter at horizon and darker overhead.

Using Color to Create Visual Depth

Our perception of the color of an object changes according to how far away the object is. In addition to looking smaller, distant objects lose some of their color intensity. There are two simple rules to follow when using color to create depth.

1. The color of an object becomes lighter and cooler as the object recedes. Because particles in the atmosphere, such as dust and vapor, obscure your vision, distant elements are not as clear as those nearby. By adding white and either gray or blue to your colors, you can get objects to recede effectively.

2. To convey vast distances between land features, you must choose fabrics with strong differences in value for those features. Conversely, if the features are close together, then the values of the corresponding fabrics must be closely aligned.

For example, when considering mountain ranges, you need to create the mountains closest to the foreground from darker, textured fabrics. Use lighter and bluer or grayer fabrics for the mountains further in the background. The color of the vegetation will also affect this phenomenon; a cleared field will read differently from a mountain covered in trees.

Depth can also be accentuated by placing the strongest sky colors visually closer to the viewer. The sky is normally a more intense color overhead and lighter near the horizon. This change of color is quite noticeable even when the sky seems at first glance to be a uniform blue.

You can further establish the illusion of depth through the use of warm and cool colors. Generally, yellow, orange, and red are considered to be warm, and blue and green are cool. Violet is more difficult to classify because it is made up of warm and cool colors and tends to change its visual temperature according to the colors around it. Surrounded by blues, violet becomes warm, whereas surrounded by reds, it seems cool.

Warm colors advance; cool colors recede.

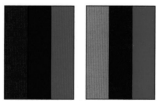

Violet surrounded by blue appears warm. Violet surrounded by red appears cool.

Placing warm colors in the foreground and cool colors in the background is another way of creating an illusion of depth. Warm colors tend to advance in comparison to cool colors. Reserve your warm colors and strong contrasts in tone for the foreground. Adding a touch of red or orange to any color will bring it forward. In contrast, adding a touch of white, blue, or green will make it recede. If you do want to use yellows, oranges, or reds in the background, you can tone them down by mixing them with their respective complementary colors or with gray.

Colors at Twilight

Sky Colors

The sky is the most magical element that enlivens any landscape. The sky's endless capacity for change makes it the most flexible element in your design. Think about interesting skies you've seen, and know that you can use one with a landscape that needs enlivening. Generally, when the sky is dramatic, it becomes the primary feature of your quilt, and all other landscape elements must support and reflect it.

When choosing the colors for your sky, look to photos for inspiration. Spectacular skies are wonderful, and you can push the colors to their limit to achieve a bold, dramatic effect. Use any color scheme to produce your own original sky. Whatever colors you choose (even green, orange, purple, or all three), when you place the sky fabric in the position of the sky in your quilt, it will read as sky. Remember that occasionally there are skies that look so surreal that you might be afraid to put them in your landscape. Take the risk. As long as the colors of the landscape work in harmony, the sky will be credible.

Before sunrise, the sky is well lit, but the colors are cool. The first rays of sunlight are the reddest, slowly shifting into orange, and gold, and eventually dazzling white. Similarly, in the hour before sunset, known to photographers as "the golden hour," the sunlight changes from white, to gold, to orange, and finally to deep red before the sun dips below the horizon. During these times, the earth is bathed in a beautiful warm glow of reflected light.

For a sunrise or sunset scene, be sure that your beautiful sky colors are echoed in your background and foreground. Although your mountains will appear to fade off into the distance, they will also take on the hue of the sky. If the sky is a deep orange, then the mountains will have an orange glow. If the sky is cream and mauve, the mountains will appear to be darker tones of purple fading off to paler mauve in the distance.

By making your far distant features a color similar to that of your sky, you can create the impression that they just gently disappear. Alternatively, when the sun has set further below the horizon, your landscape features might stand out as a dark silhouette.

Water Colors

Water has no color of its own, but it reflects the colors of the elements around it. There's the deep blue ocean, the turquoise of a Caribbean lagoon, the red-orange seascape at sunset, and, strangest of all, a perfectly clear glass of water. The main source of water's color is the sky, although water is usually darker in tone than the sky. Water is usually lighter in color near the horizon and more intense in color as it approaches the foreground.

Glitter Patterns on the Water—Pathway to the Moon

Looking toward the sun's or moon's reflection across a broad stretch of wind-ruffled water, we sometimes see a brilliant elongated path of sparkling light called glitter. This glitter may extend from the horizon directly below the sun almost to our feet. As the sun approaches the horizon, the glitter becomes narrower, and it disappears completely when the sun is on the horizon. This

Inspirational sunset

First rays of sunlight in early morning

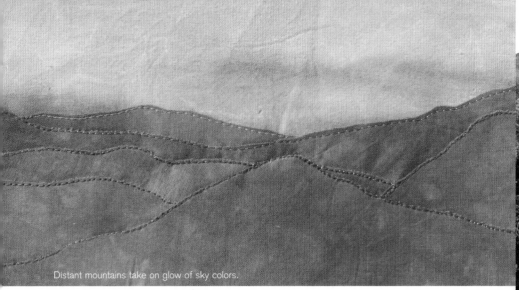

Distant mountains take on glow of sky colors.

Land bathed in warm glow of evening light

spectacular light show is orchestrated by millions of sun glints, each reflected from a wave with just the right slope and position to send the light our way.

Silhouettes

Shapes, such as trees and buildings, become silhouettes when juxtaposed against stunning twilight skies. Rather than use pure black fabric, create your silhouettes in shades such as dark gray, deep indigo, teal, navy blue, and so on. A fabric that is dark but slightly mottled in texture can be more effective than a flat, plain color.

You may find that some of the key elements of your composition disappear when they are against a dark background. If so, you may need to reverse the dark/light effect partway up. For example, a yacht's mast that is light against a dark dock may have to be changed to dark where it reaches the sky. A tree trunk may need to be light against the dark water but darker against the light sky. This reversal may sound strange, but it does work visually.

Finally, remember that if you really want to enjoy your beautiful sky, keep the foreground simple. You don't want the two elements fighting for pride of place.

Keep your color wheel handy as you select your fabrics. It is a wonderful reference point. You should also visit museums and galleries and look at how other artists approach color. Learn from the masters!

The 3-in-1 Color Tool is a color-planning tool that can help you choose effective combinations.

Sparkling glitter on water

photograph to design

Tidal Images, 100″ × 82″ (250cm × 205cm), Gloria Loughman

Using a Camera

Beyond its own intrinsic value as a fine art form, photography is a valuable tool for an artist. A camera can record a lot of information easily and quickly, saving images that the eye and memory cannot. Photographs can capture the delicate patterns of veins in a leaf, provide a reference for the wings of a bird in flight, record the stunning color changes of the sky at sunset, or monitor the ebb and flow of the restless sea.

In the art world, the use of cameras is sometimes ridiculed as cheating or inhibiting creativity. Setting up an easel *en plein air* (outdoors, on location) is often advocated as the only way to truly capture a scene. But we quilters employ a much longer process, and although we would sometimes love to work outdoors, the practicalities of stitching on a machine render this impossible. We don't have the luxury of time to sit outdoors, gazing at the beautiful scene before us as we carefully choose our fabrics, cut out our pieces, and then accurately stitch them together.

Take Control

To ensure that your work is fresh and lively, you must combine the technical information recorded in photographs with your own interpretation and feelings. One of the pitfalls is to copy a photograph just as it is; and with the high depth of field achieved with cameras, you can easily be overwhelmed with detail. Ignore the details and don't hesitate to leave out elements or move them around. Sometimes a tree moved, or even eliminated, or a mountain shape slightly enlarged or reduced, can improve your composition.

Don't Leave Home Without Your Camera

Get into the habit of taking your camera everywhere with you. You never know when a photo opportunity will arise. It may be that magnificent sculptured dead tree on your way to the train station or the stunning fields of golden flowers by the side of the highway. Be observant as you travel around. Build up your library of photographs alongside your sketches and other resources. You can even use your camera to compose your own design—the viewfinder makes a good picture finder.

Learn to take your own photographs because copying pictures from books, magazines, or other published materials is illegal, unless the material is specifically designated as copyright-free.

Working From Photos

Back at home, you can spread out your photos for consideration. The appeal of images that visually excite you can be translated to your audience. Work from more than one photograph even if you don't plan to include all the information. This way you will know your subject better because you'll have a record of the colors and a selection of features as a point of reference. Memories of special places are evoked easily, and looking at your photos will usually prompt a collage of ideas.

The Process

Your first task should be to establish a focal point and determine its place within the framework of your design. Now play with the composition. In all likelihood, your reference photos will not be works of art as they are. It's rare that every element of the subject will be exactly where you want it. A tree branch may lead the viewer's eye out of the picture or cut across the focal point. Buildings may be too parallel to one another or too monotonous in shape or size, or there may be a crowd of distracting elements in the background or foreground. Eliminate unessential details. Add trees, fences, people, and so on from other sources if necessary.

Emphasize interesting shapes or move them closer to the foreground. Try scaling down or simplifying other elements.

Experiment with different times of the day, or even different seasons. Use a photo taken in the morning to create a night scene. Ask yourself questions like "What if the sky were scarlet?" When you give yourself permission to make changes, the possibilities are endless.

Once you have sketched your design, experiment with color. Photocopy your sketches and try shading them with paint, pastels, or pencils, using different color combinations. Choose the color scheme that speaks to you, the one that sets the mood you want to portray.

Consider changing the direction of your light source by exploring the light shining on your subject from several different directions. Thus, even poorly lit photos can become beautiful landscapes.

Finally, put away all your reference photos and keep playing with your composition and colors. For the photographer, the image obtained is the finished product. For you, the photos are only a starting place and a reference. Trust yourself to be inventive. You will never grow as an artist if you only copy exactly what the camera records. You must let the subject speak to you. You are a special person with a unique way of seeing the world. The more you bring of yourself—your creativity and your own spirit—to creating from photos, the more exciting your work will be.

Example 1: Lighthouse at Point Hicks

Original photo provides inspiration.

Main lines traced to ensure perspective

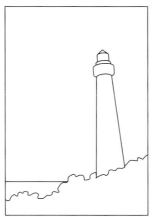

Foreground line redrawn to allow for area of sea

Sunset at Point Hicks,
$14\frac{1}{2}'' \times 19\frac{1}{2}''$ (37cm × 50cm),
Gloria Loughman

Finished quilt. Note shading on side of lighthouse; texture and color are gained through machine embroidery in foreground.

Example 2: Gregory National Park

Original photo provides inspiration.

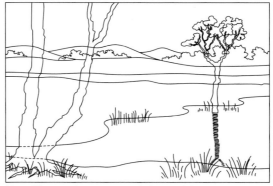

Note differences between original photo and drawing.

Example 3: Loddon River

Original photo taken at sunset

Second photo taken later in evening further downstream

Finished quilt includes elements of both photos.

Loddon River Tranquility,
$15'' \times 22''$ (38cm × 56cm),
Gloria Loughman

painting landscape fabric

Golden Dreaming, 64″ × 96″ (160cm × 240cm), Gloria Loughman

Photo by Sharon Risedorph

Equipment

Transparent Fabric Paint

There are quite a few fabric paints on the market. I live in Australia, so the one I find the cheapest and easiest to obtain is Hi Strike, sold by Batik Oetoro in Sydney. In the United States, Setacolor is the fabric paint of choice, and Silhouette is popular in New Zealand. All are transparent fabric paints. They leave the fabric feeling soft, and they can be diluted considerably for color washes. These paints work well on cotton and silk and are permanent when dried and set with heat.

Usually you have to water down the paint you use for skies. The amount of water needed varies depending on the brand and the intensity of the color you want. A good starting point is one part paint to two or three parts water.

Opaque Paint

Along with transparent fabric paints, small amounts of opaque paint are also useful to have on hand when you need to apply paint that stays on the surface. You can use opaque fabric paints such as Setacolor opaque or Neopaque (in the United States) or regular artists' acrylic paint. White is the obvious choice because it can be mixed with transparent fabric paint to give you a range of paler colors. Also, it is the light color that you'll need, for example, to paint snow on a dark mountain top or whitecaps on a stormy sea. Thin acrylic paint with water to avoid stiffness and set it with heat.

Brushes

Brushes are available for a huge variety of prices and purposes. Sponge brushes are excellent, inexpensive tools because they absorb a large quantity of paint and are easy to use. They come in various widths with a blade-shaped foam head. They can be used to apply a smooth wide layer of paint or to create a fine narrow line with their sharp edges.

Regular paintbrushes come in a range of sizes and types. Most paints are applied with a sponge brush, so you need just a few other brushes for special effects. They include stencil, fan, square, and pointed brushes.

A good, wide soft-bristle brush can also be handy. The key to selecting brushes is to choose ones that are large enough to hold an adequate amount of paint.

Sponges

Available from art, craft, and hardware stores, sponges are a wonderful tool for applying foliage, adding texture to rocks, and touching up clouds.

Supplies

Fabric

White cotton fabric is an excellent choice for fabric painting, although any fabric can be painted. White fabric as a starting point gives you a more accurate color than beige or cream fabric. You don't need to prewash your fabric before you paint unless it has a finish that prevents the paint from sinking in. If in doubt, prewash, or use prepared-for-dyeing (PFD) fabric.

Painting Surface

Plastic-covered foamcore board or lightweight white melamine boards are excellent flat surfaces to spread your fabric on. These can be positioned on your table for painting and then placed in a sunny spot on your lawn or porch while the fabric dries. Alternatively, you can spread out sheets of plastic, or you may even be tempted to paint fabric directly on your tabletop. The paint will easily wash off solid surfaces. Be aware of what is under your fabric as it is drying. Wrinkles or creases in plastic will result in white lines on your fabric. Likewise, if you put your fabric to dry on grass, bricks, or stones, you will get patterns in your fabric. In some cases you can use this to your advantage, but if that's not what you want, be sure your painting and drying surfaces are smooth.

TIP

If you're going to use plastic, spray your work surface (table or foamcore) with a little water before laying down the plastic. The water will help hold the plastic to the surface without wrinkles or creases.

Painting Skies

The English painter John Constable (1776–1837) once said, "The sky is the source of nature's light: it rules the entire landscape."

Nothing is more thrilling and visually stimulating than watching a spectacular sunset, whether it is over the ocean, from the top of a mountain, or in the flat desert land, where the skies seem so much bigger.

The secret of painting sky fabric is to start with some simple skies and gradually work your way up to the more dramatic ones. Observe skies and see how they are structured. Look at the colors, shapes, and tones.

The behavior of fabric paint when it is applied to wet fabric lends itself to sky painting. The unpredictability of wet washes on the wet fabric, the transparency of the medium, and the possibility of coming up with an exciting accident all contribute to the range of effects that can be achieved.

Sunsets can be breathtaking.

Sunset and Sunrise Skies

Breathtaking winter sunsets often incorporate the spectacular bold colors of violet, deep blue, magenta, red, orange, yellow, and gold. When the sky puts on a dramatic spectacle, the colors are often strong and include some pure hues as well as shades and tones. Create shades by adding a small amount of black. Create tones by adding gray or the complement of the pure color. Begin with your selected color and add small amounts of gray or black until you have the color you want.

In contrast, summer sunsets are generally less bold and often feature the softer tones and tints of cream, rose, lavender, apricot, and light blue. A soft, tinted palette can be made by starting with white and adding the selected colors in very small amounts. In addition, watering down the paints can also give you pale colors.

When painting sunsets, remember to decide on the position of the sun. When the sun is going down below the clouds, they will appear lighter below and darker above. When the sun is hidden, clouds appear flatter, with less contrast of tone.

Start a sunrise or sunset at the sun and work outward, layering the colors into one another. Vary the colors as you proceed, for example, adding crimson to yellow, then blue to crimson, and finally returning to the sun to add highlights of pale lemon.

Clouds

If you want to make clouds the focal point of your composition, give them ample room by lowering the horizon line. Sometimes the appeal of a subject is the scale of the sky compared to the landscape. Keep cloud shapes simple and varied. Manipulate the shape, size, and color of the clouds to exaggerate what you want to convey.

Create movement by placing clouds in diagonals across the sky, rather than arranging them in horizontal lines. Alternatively, horizontal clouds can be used to indicate calm.

Diagonal clouds create movement.

Be aware that clouds are rarely pure white. If you look carefully, you'll see that they have all sorts of pale tints. White looks rather dull and lifeless, whereas pale colors make the clouds look more believable and give them greater depth. In addition to highlights, look for lovely warm or cool shadows with real color, not just gray. Clouds are often actually purple or blue.

Clouds take many forms and shapes, but no matter what kind of clouds they are, the laws of perspective apply. Clouds are smaller the further away they are, so to create depth, paint them smaller as they near the horizon. Remember that some forms of clouds have flat bottoms.

Clouds get smaller in distance; sky is more intense in color overhead.

Applying the Paint

1. Dilute the paint, mixing approximately two parts water to one part paint. The proportions will vary, of course, depending on the depth of the color you want to use.

2. Moisten the fabric by spraying it with water or submerging it in a container of water. Stretch the fabric over your painting surface, easing out air bubbles and removing loose threads. (Note: These threads can create wonderful lightning effects if left on the fabric; when they are removed at the end of the drying process, their white image is left behind. See page 33.)

3. Apply the diluted color with foam brushes or a sponge. Dabbing creates texture, and long strokes produce smooth color. Begin with the lightest colors first, laying down a basic wash of paint and blending the colors. Most people find it easier to paint from the horizon upward. You can always go darker, but sometimes it is difficult using transparent paint to go lighter. Then it's time to go back over areas to create highlights and contrasts.

Begin with lightest colors first, laying down basic wash.

Add more intense color.

Go back over areas, creating depth.

4. Apply details with a fine brush. The fantail brush works well for bolder fine lines.

Apply paint with sponge brush to produce smooth color.

Add cloud details with fantail brush.

5. Use a spray bottle to add extra moisture if you want the colors to really flow into each other. Don't overdo it though, or you may be left with a pale all-over wash.

6. If the weather is warm, you can also use your spray bottle to prevent the sky fabric from drying out before you have finished. If you need to, you can let your fabric dry and then wet it again by brushing on clear water.

7. After you have finished painting, place your stretched fabric in the sun to dry. When left in bright sunshine, the colors will dry brighter than applied. (It is for this reason that I sometimes dry my more sub- dued pieces overnight.)

8. Once the fabric is dry, remove it from its base and iron it for 2 minutes on the back side. Try to allow at least 48 hours after ironing before washing by hand in warm water. After you dry and press the fabric, it is ready to use.

Soft pastel sky

Sky with contrasting colors

Very pale sky

Sky in complementary tones

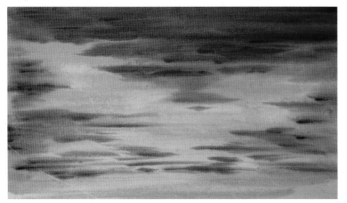
Sky in analogous tones

Wet Paint on Wet Fabric

As you are applying wet paint to wet fabric, sometimes an accident will result in something special. The nature of the wet fabric allows fluid runs and exciting mixtures of color. Sometimes you just have to let nature take over and let the paint do its own thing without a heavy hand messing it up. Give your imagination full rein, using a light touch and allowing for spontaneity.

To further explore the fluidity of wet paint, try tilting your board as the fabric is drying. Keep an eye on how far the paint is running because you might need to lay the board flat after a period of time.

Special Skies

Some skies are so dramatic that they need special treatment. Rather than starting with a wash of color, you may need to paint in some of the features first to give yourself a structure or reference to work with. You can then go back and fill in the spaces with beautiful color.

Begin by painting in basic structure.

Fill in with background wash and details.

Tilt board to encourage paint to run.

Sometimes back of fabric is better than front.

Strong sky

Paler version on back side

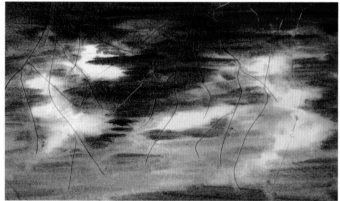

Place threads on painted surface before drying.

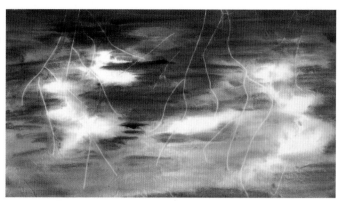

Remove threads to create lightning.

Become a student of the sky. Skies are constantly changing, sometimes dramatic, sometimes tranquil. Let the flow of paint take you along with it. Allow yourself to be free flowing and relaxed about it.

Painting Other Areas of the Landscape

Water

It is important at all times to reinforce the impression that water is hori–zontal. Even when water is broken by waves, it is still basically a flat plane. Lines or elements that make water look like it is going up-hill must be avoided at all costs. Use a large brush and apply horizontal brushstrokes.

Paint sky first; then mirror in water using darker colors.

Water has no color of its own, and its surface will reflect the sky and the objects around it. Generally, it will be darker than the sky. There are also other factors that affect the color, including the depth of the water. There can be quite dark purplish patches caused by reefs, and yellow-green patches created by sand beneath the surface.

To achieve perspective, paint the water lighter in tone near the horizon and darker as the water approaches the foreground.

Align water and sky fabric for accurate placement of reflected light.

Land

To paint fabric for the darkened land at twilight, lay down an undercoat of the sky color, and paint over the surface in a darker hue, leaving small areas of color showing through to help unite areas. Add texture with a brush or sponge to create grasses or ploughed fields.

More Fun With Fabric Paint

The properties of transparent fabric paints make them suitable for heliographic (or sun) fabric art. This simple process allows you to create images on fabric. Place objects such as leaves, mesh, cardboard shapes, shells, lace, buttons, feathers, netting, and flowers on the surface of the fabric after you have applied the paint and it is still wet. Allow the fabric to dry in the sun. When the fabric is dry, remove the objects, and their images will remain. The area under the object dries lighter than the rest (rather than darker) because the paint reacts with the light to set it.

Creating Textured Fabrics

Scrunching or creasing the fabric when it is wet, and then applying the paint, can produce some interesting textures. Allow extra drying time for scrunched fabric.

Leaves leave image on wet painted fabric.

preparing to stitch

Sewing Machine

The most important feature of a sewing machine is its operator. I have worked with students who have brought to class an old machine that has been cherished and lovingly cared for. They coax and cajole it along, producing absolutely impeccable stitching. Nevertheless, my advice is to buy the best machine you can afford. Do your research to make sure that the machine you are considering can be adjusted to produce the stitching you require. Read your machine manual to find out what your machine is capable of, and then try it, play with it, use it, and challenge it to work for you.

Feed Dogs

The feed dogs, as the name suggests, feed the fabric through the machine at a certain stitch length in a straight line. At times, you will need to drop or cover your feed dogs to allow easier movement of your work. Check your machine manual for instructions on how to lower or cover the feed dogs. If you can't lower the feed dogs, and your machine doesn't come with an accessory to cover them, tape a business card over them, making a hole for the needle to pass through.

Sewing Machine Feet

Darning Foot

The darning foot has a hopping action that causes the foot to move up and down when the machine is stitching, allowing room for you to move the fabric and freely work in any direction. Darning feet can be made of metal or plastic, and they vary in design with each brand. Some manufacturers make a darning foot that is open in front for better visibility of your stitching.

Walking Foot

The walking foot is wonderful for quilting straight lines and gentle curves, for quilting in-the-ditch, and for attaching bindings. The walking foot allows all layers of a quilt sandwich to move along together through the machine. This foot prevents the top layer from shifting or stretching during quilting.

Open Embroidery Foot

The open embroidery foot allows you to see your stitching and provides a clear view of an edge to be satin stitched, or of a pattern to be followed. This foot is used with the feed dogs in the up position. Another alternative is a clear plastic foot that also allows good visibility; use this foot for satin stitching, invisible blind hemming, and some of the decorative stitches.

Darning foot

Open embroidery foot with good visibility

Walking foot

Sewing Machine Needles

Many types of sewing machine needles are available today, and selecting the right needle is critical. Many of the needles have been developed for specific purposes and are available in different sizes.

Most needle sizes are indicated by two numbers separated by a slash, for example, 80/12 or 90/14. The higher number refers to the European metric size, and the lower number is the American size. Needles range in size from very fine (60/8) to heavy duty (120/19). Choose the needle size to match your thread. If you use a large needle with a fine thread, your quilt will have thousands of small holes that are not filled up with thread. If the needle is too small, your thread will shred and break.

If you are using a very fine thread, such as size 60 cotton, nylon, or MonoPoly, select a size 60/8 needle. This needle will make a tiny hole and is perfect for invisible blind hemming. Take care, though; the needle is so fine that it is quite fragile and easily broken.

For piecing, size 70/10 needles are great, especially the Jeans (Denim) needle, which has a sharp point.

I use topstitch needles for machine embroidery, size 80/12 for my 40-weight threads, and size 90/14 for my 30-weight and metallic threads. The topstitch needle has an extra-large eye and a much deeper groove to protect the thread as it passes through the fabric to join the bobbin thread.

The new 20- and 12-weight threads need a needle with a still larger eye, so consider the 100/16 for these threads.

When your machine makes a dull clunking noise as you stitch, it is likely that a needle change is long overdue. Always change your needle after approximately eight hours of stitching because needles become blunt and dull even with normal sewing. Some good advice I heard recently was to always start a new project with a new needle.

Threads

Many quilters today are as addicted to collecting threads as they are to collecting fabric. There are so many wonderful threads to choose from that sometimes knowing where to start is difficult.

Thread Weight

Just as needles come in different sizes, so does thread; but just to keep you on your toes, the sizing goes in the reverse direction. The higher the number, the finer the thread. A 40-weight thread is finer than a 30-weight thread.

For me, the most important factors when choosing thread for embroidery are color and weight. If you want the thread to blend in, choose a finer weight. If you want the stitching to stand out or fill in areas of color, choose a thicker thread.

Rayon

Rayon threads are soft and have an attractive sheen. They can be difficult to use because they break easily, so make sure you use a topstitch needle to alleviate this drawback. Madeira and Sulky make an attractive range of colors in both the 40-weight and the heavier 30-weight threads.

Polyester

Like rayon threads, many polyester threads also have a high sheen, but polyester is easier to use because it is stronger and more durable. Among my favorites are the trilobal polyesters made by Superior Threads that flow through my sewing machine at a great rate without mishap.

Polyester and rayon threads

Cotton

Good-quality cotton thread is a joy to use, but be wary of cheaper brands because they tend to create lint in your sewing machine. Cotton thread is great for piecing, and there are some wonderful decorative variegated threads made by Superior, Signature, Sulky, and Valdani for machine quilting and embroidery.

Cotton thread

Pearle Cotton

Some threads are too thick to go through the needle. This group of threads includes the thicker Pearle cotton and rayon threads with sizes ranging from 3 to 12. Valdani makes a beautiful range of variegated Pearle cottons in sizes 8 and 12. These thicker threads need to be wound on a bobbin and sewn from the back side of the work.

Thicker threads

Monofilament

Monofilament thread is a good option for invisible machine appliqué. Wonder Invisible thread by YLI (size .004) was my preferred option for many years because it is fine and not too stiff and springy. However, I recently discovered MonoPoly, manufac-

tured by Superior Threads, and have switched to using it. It is also size .004 and is made of polyester rather than nylon, which means that it is heat resistant and strong but still soft and pliable. Although both of these threads make color matching a certainty, I prefer not to use them for quilting because I don't like the plastic glint you get when the stitching catches the light. Both the Wonder Invisible thread and MonoPoly are available in smoke color for stitching dark colors and clear for light fabrics.

Monofilament thread

Bobbin Thread

In recent years, a number of threads have been developed specifically for the bobbin, including Bobbinfil (Mettler) and Bottom Line (Superior). These soft, fine threads allow you to wind a large amount of thread on bobbins, and their soft finish allows them to slide over rather than grab the top thread. I like to use these threads in the bobbin for satin stitching and machine embroidery to avoid getting a buildup of thread underneath my work.

Specialty fine bobbin threads

My early hand-sewing experiences in high school left me with a dread of attempting anything by hand, although I do painstakingly hand stitch my bindings down to complete my quilts. Actually, I invite the same three friends over for supper each time a large quilt is close to completion. We each take one side and carefully stitch down the binding. With the promise of some high-calorie treats and lubricating fluids, we stitch away enthusiastically, laughing and reminiscing about previous quilts and events.

The projects featured later in the book can all be completed using hand stitching if you like, but I will leave it to the experts to provide the descriptions of the invisible hand appliqué and quilting techniques to be employed. Here, I'll focus on using a sewing machine.

Tension

I really enjoy stitching on my sewing machine, although I know for some people, machine sewing can be a never-ending source of frustration. The source of most aggravation is thread tension. With a thorough understanding and mastering of tension, you will be able to use various weights of thread, experiment with different stitches, and complete your projects with an excellent degree of workmanship.

When, filled with excitement and anticipation, you unpack your new sewing machine, you will find that it has been preset to make perfect stitches on the top and bottom of your work. Even when the top thread is red and the bobbin thread is blue, you can see perfect red stitches on the top and neat blue ones underneath. That is, of course, as long as the red and blue threads are identical in weight and composition. However, if you are brave enough to use a metallic thread on the top and a polyester thread in the bobbin, you might run into problems. To be able to vary your threads and get the best performance from your machine, you must adjust your tension settings.

Bobbin Tension

It is worth checking your bobbin tension before starting to stitch. If the bobbin tension is correct, then all other adjustments can be made by adjusting the top tension up or down.

With the bobbin correctly inserted in its case (check your manual to see if the bobbin should spin clockwise or counterclockwise), let the bobbin case hang down freely by the thread. It must not slide down under its own weight, but when you jerk your hand gently upward, yo-yo style, the bobbin should fall slowly. If it doesn't move at all, the tension is too tight. If it falls easily, the tension is too loose. Adjust the tension by turning the screw on the tension clip. Using the tiny screwdriver that came with your sewing machine, turn the screw to the right to tighten, and to the left to loosen. Adjust in tiny increments until the tension is correct. Think of the screw as the face of a clock, and move only five minutes at a time.

Adjusting the bobbin tension

If you change the weight of thread in your bobbin, you should recheck the tension. Very fine specialty bobbin threads such as Bottom Line (Superior Threads) or Bobbinfil (Mettler) will require a tighter bobbin tension. Likewise, if you use a heavy thread, the bobbin tension will need to be loosened. If you find yourself frequently having to adjust your bobbin tension for these threads, then a second bobbin case, clearly marked so you don't confuse it with your regular bobbin case, is an excellent investment.

If your machine doesn't have a removable bobbin case, you can still fine-tune the tension by adjusting the screw that is usually situated in the center front of the bobbin housing. The same rules apply—turn the screw to the right to tighten and to the left to loosen.

Top Tension

Once you have your bobbin tension correct, thread your machine with your chosen thread and stitch a few inches on a small sample to see whether you need to adjust the top tension. If you can see any of the bobbin thread coming through to the top of the fabric, your top tension is too tight. Lower the tension by adjusting the top tension dial to a lower number. For example, if the dial was set at 4, turn it to 3.5 and stitch another sample. If you can still see the bobbin thread coming through to the top, try 3. Keep lowering the setting until you are happy with the stitch, both top and bottom. Some older machines have a tension dial that displays a + symbol and a – symbol instead of numbers. To loosen the upper tension on these machines, adjust the dial to the negative side.

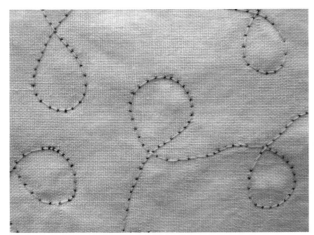

Bobbin thread showing through to top—top tension is too tight

On the other hand, if you get a straight line of thread on the back of your sample, the top thread is too loose. To fix this problem, tighten the top tension. If the dial is set on 4, try 4.5. Check the stitching again, and if you can't see neat stitches on the back, try 5. You are aiming to have neat, perfect stitches on both sides of your work. Correct tension is particularly important when you are quilting because both sides of the decorative stitching will be on show. If it is just impossible to get the perfect stitch, top and bottom, you should match the color of your bobbin thread with that of your top thread. Then, if the bobbin thread does show slightly on the top, it will blend in and not be apparent.

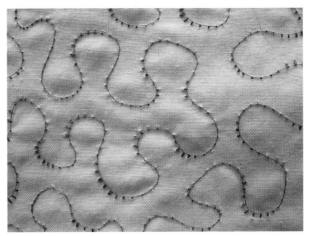

Bobbin thread forms straight line on back—top tension is too loose

The type of fabric, the thickness of your batting, and the thickness and type of your upper and lower thread can affect stitching. With all these variables, understanding tension and knowing how to adjust it are crucial.

Machine Appliqué

A number of techniques can be used to secure appliquéd pieces in place. Smaller pieces can be fused in place and then stitched down around the edges so they are held permanently in position.

Using Fusible Web

For raw-edge or satin-stitch appliqué, use paper-backed fusible web, such as Wonder Under (in the United States) or Vliesofix (Australia, New Zealand, and Europe), remembering that to avoid getting a mirror image of your motif, you must reverse the motif or trace from the back of the original pattern. A light-box is a valuable tool because you can place your pattern right side down on the box and easily trace the visible reverse image onto your fusible web.

TIP

A cheaper alternative to a lightbox is to tape your pattern to a window or glass door and then trace the visible reverse image on the back of your pattern onto fusible web.

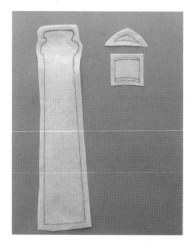

1. Trace motif on smooth side of web; then cut out motif, leaving a small margin around outside of shape.

2. Use dry iron on medium heat setting to iron web onto back of fabric.

3. Cut out shapes, adding extra fabric to tuck under where necessary. Peel off backing paper, change iron setting to steam, and fuse shapes to background.

4. Stitch around edge with narrow satin or straight stitch.

Satin-Stitch Appliqué

Satin stitching completely encloses raw edges and has a crisp, stable finish that provides a well-defined edge. Use a zigzag stitch with the stitch length set very short, so that the stitches sit snugly, right up next to each other. Pieces are first fused to the background so they don't shift during stitching.

Preparing for Satin Stitching

1. To ensure that the stitches sit flat, always back your work with a fabric stabilizer, such as a tear-away product, to avoid puckering.

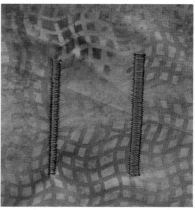

Stitching on left was done without stabilizer.

2. Prepare your fabric pieces to be stitched by following the instructions for fusible web outlined above.

3. Choose a needle that is appropriate for your thread size. Ideally you want the smallest needle possible, so that the holes made by the needle will be filled with thread.

4. Choose a foot that allows you to see where you are going. The open-toe embroidery foot is my preferred option. A clear plastic foot that allows you to see your work as you stitch is a good alternative.

5. Select the zigzag setting and adjust your stitch width to approximately 2. This width setting will vary, depending on the size of the motif being appliquéd. For a large motif, a wider stitch of perhaps 3 or more would be appropriate. For tiny pieces, a stitch width of 1 would be suitable.

6. Thread your machine with thread that matches the color of your motif: 40-weight rayon or polyester machine embroidery threads are both excellent for satin stitch because they seem to sit flatter than some of the other threads available. For most projects, it is important to get as close a color match to your fabric as possible to ensure that the thread blends with the fabric rather than stands out around the edge.

7. Make sure that your bobbin thread is wound smoothly and evenly. You can use a fine special-purpose bobbin thread or a polyester thread in a color similar to your top thread. Don't try to save money by using a lower-quality thread in the bobbin. Doing so is likely to cause you all kinds of problems because these threads tend to be uneven and quite thick. For satin stitching, use a bobbin thread that is equal in weight to or finer than the top thread.

8. Check the tension. When you are trying to achieve a perfect satin stitch, the top thread should be pulled down to the underside; thus, the bobbin tension should be fairly tight and the top tension slightly loosened. Check your bobbin tension first to make sure that it is firm and not too loose. If you are using a Bernina sewing machine, thread the bobbin thread through the finger on the bobbin case to further tighten the bobbin tension. Then adjust your top tension down to a lower number, for example, from 5 to 4. Practice on a sample of fabric backed with stabilizer.

When you check the underside of your work, the top thread should look like railroad tracks on either side of the bobbin thread. If the top thread is not visible, or if any of the bobbin thread is showing on the top, loosen the top tension further and try again. When changing threads, you will need to recheck your tension by stitching on your sample.

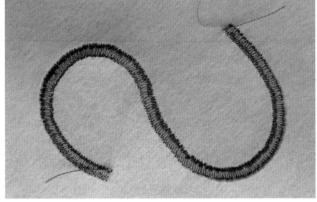
Practice on a sample. On back, top thread looks like railroad tracks.

9. Adjust the stitch length. You are aiming to have your stitches as close together as possible, while still allowing the work to move freely through the machine without being pushed. The stitch length will probably be in the vicinity of .25 to .5. You should also check the stitch width and length on your sample before you set to work on the real thing. Although this testing takes time, in the long run you will save hours of frustration caused by having to pick out stitches because the stitching is not good enough.

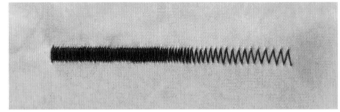
Aim to have stitches close together, like those at left.

T I P

Use scraps of your motif fabric so you can check the color of the thread as well as the tension.

Satin Stitching

1. Start stitching on a straight section of the motif because it is easier to get a feel for where you are heading and you can disguise your start and finish points more easily. To start, take one stitch and then pull on the top thread to bring the bobbin thread up to the top of your work. Then stitch around the motif. Most of each stitch should fall on the piece being appliquéd rather than on the background. You should always aim to have your stitches at a 90° angle to the edge of your motif, turning the work slowly but evenly as you proceed. Try to keep sewing for long runs, gradually rotating your work rather then starting and stopping.

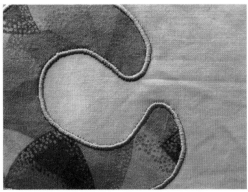
Aim to have stitches at 90° angle to edge.

2. When you reach the point where you do need to change the angle to go around a tight curve, stop your machine with the needle down in the fabric on the outside of the curve. Lift the presser foot, turn the fabric slightly, and then lower the foot and sew a few more stitches. Continue in this way, sewing, stopping, pivoting, sewing, and so on until the curve is completed. If you stop on the inside of a curve and pivot, you will get small gaps in your stitching.

3. If you have to sew around a corner or point, you have several alternatives, as shown below.

For wide corners, stitch right to end; then overlap in new direction.

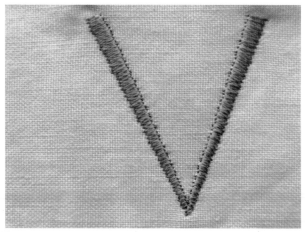

For narrow points, gradually decrease stitch width as you approach point, stop with needle down, pivot work, and then increase width in new direction.

4. When you have returned to your starting point, overlap by two or three stitches. Change the needle position to the right, set the stitch width to 0, and take several small stitches. Tie off the threads at the back of the work to finish. If you are stopping at the edge of

another fabric, stitch three or four stitches into the next fabric, stop, and then tie off the threads on the back. When you stitch the next fabric, these stitches will be covered.

Raw-Edge Appliqué

In contrast to satin stitching, raw-edge appliqué involves free-motion stitching around the motif once, or a number of times, to capture the threads; it is more subtle and less defined. Free-motion stitching requires you to drop or cover your feed dogs so you can move the fabric in any direction. Mastering this technique opens up a whole new world of stitching possibilities, not just for appliqué but for machine embroidery and quilting as well. You will need to practice, of course, but your endeavors will be rewarded with wonderful results.

Preparing for Raw-Edge Appliqué

1. Attach your darning foot. Drop or cover your feed dogs and release the presser foot if necessary. Adjust your stitch width and length to 0. For free-motion stitching, you need a fairly tight bobbin tension and a slightly loosened top tension. To achieve the correct top tension, adjust the setting down one or two numbers. If you can still see your bobbin thread peeping through to the top of your work, continue reducing the top tension until the bobbin thread disappears.

2. Make a practice sample of fabric pinned to a piece of stabilizer. Place your fabric under the darning foot. To start, take one stitch and pull the top thread to bring the bobbin thread up to the top of your work. Lower the needle into the work, and, if possible, set the machine to the needle-down position.

3. Gently press on the foot pedal while steadily moving the fabric. Just think of the needle as a pencil that is fixed in position while you are moving the paper underneath it to draw a pattern. When you first try this technique, you will feel a little out of control, but hang in there. It is the most liberating and exciting technique to master. Try drawing a few circles and then draw some flowers or leaves. Try writing your name and the names of others in your family.

Have fun drawing with thread.

Remember that you are in control of moving the fabric—you have taken on the role of the feed dogs. If you move the fabric slowly, you will get tiny stitches. If you move it quickly, you will get large stitches. If you don't move it at all, you will get a buildup of stitches on one spot. You have to balance the stitching speed of the machine, which is maintained by your pressure on the foot pedal, and the speed at which you move the fabric. Some people prefer to run both the machine and the fabric at a high speed. Others proceed slowly, even setting their machine to a lower speed, if that is an option. Everyone has an optimum speed that gives the greatest control. Personally, I am one of the slower, more cautious stitchers. With lots of practice, you will settle into a rhythm that gives you the best results and affords you greater control.

Once you feel reasonably confident stitching patterns, try stitching around fused shapes.

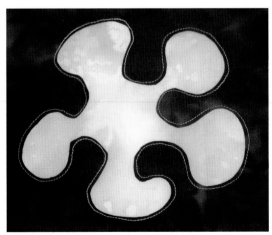
Practice on sample, trying to stitch close to edge.

Raw-Edge Stitching

1. Fuse your fabric shapes to your quilt top.

2. Thread your machine with a thread that is as close as possible in color to the motif fabric. Your bobbin thread can be matching or neutral in color.

3. Back the fabric to be stitched with tear-away stabilizer. Place the fabric under the darning foot and follow the procedure described above to get started. Remember to move the fabric gently and evenly to get uniform stitches. Proceed around the outside edge of your motif, trying to stitch $\frac{1}{16}''$ (2mm) from the fused edge. Secure the thread ends by tying them off on the back.

You will find that some fabrics fray more than others. Batiks, which have a high thread count, are less likely to fray than an open-weave fabric.

Second row of stitching helps prevent fraying in **Kimberley Mystique** (page 6).

Three-Dimensional Appliqué

Now that you have mastered satin stitching and free-motion stitching, you can create three-dimensional shapes that can be attached to the quilt surface. This method is useful for making flowers, leaves, butterflies, and so on that you attach to the surface to create depth and interest.

1. Choose fabrics for the top and bottom layers of your motif and gather together your fusible web and stabilizer. You are going to create a sandwich of fabric, fusible web, and stabilizer. Cut a square of the top and bottom fabrics, 2 squares of fusible web, and 1 square of stabilizer. Press the fusible web squares onto the wrong sides of the fabric squares. Then remove the backing paper from the fusible web, place the stabilizer between the fused fabric squares, and fuse all the layers together with a hot iron.

2. Trace your appliqué shape onto the dull side of freezer paper and iron the shape onto the top fabric of the sandwich.

Iron freezer-paper shapes onto sandwich.

3. Cut around the edge of the freezer paper, cutting through all the layers. Remove the freezer paper. Shapes such as leaves can be cut freehand, directly from the sandwich.

4. Place the cut-out shape on another piece of tear-away stabilizer and satin stitch around the shape, keeping the stitches mainly on the piece being appliquéd.

Satin stitch around leaves backed with stabilizer.

5. Gently tear away the stabilizer from the stitching. You may need to use tweezers or small scissors. Be careful that you don't put too much pressure on the stitches. Rubbing a damp finger along the edge of the stitching will remove most of the tiny pieces of stabilizer.

6. Use free-motion stitching to stitch the motif into place on your quilt surface. Shading lines or veins can be added at this stage. Stitch the center of the shape rather than the outside edge so the motif stands out from the background.

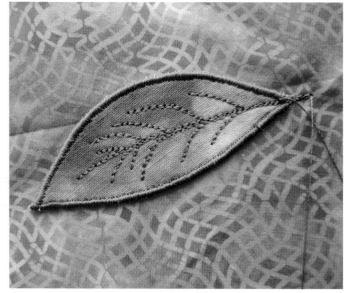
Attach by stitching veins of leaf through to quilt top.

Three-dimensional monstera leaves in **Bingil Bay** (page 4)

Invisible Appliqué

I use invisible appliqué to sew most of my background pieces together. This technique allows you to overlap pieces, with the edge of the top fabric pressed under. You can manipulate the pieces into the best position, pin them in place, and then stitch without having a visible line of thread. I also use this technique to appliqué some of the larger shapes to the quilt surface, especially those that look better without an obvious stitching line.

Invisible appliqué uses a blind hem stitch. (Consult your sewing machine manual if necessary to see whether your machine has this stitch.) The blind hem stitch consists of four to seven straight stitches followed by a zigzag to the left. On some machines, you can get a mirror image of the stitch to sew the opposite way.

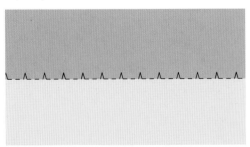

Blind hem stitch

Preparing for Invisible Appliqué

1. Use a foot that is open at the front or use a clear appliqué foot to give you the best view. Your sewing machine manual may advise you to use the specialized blind hem foot, but ignore that advice because that foot turns under the top edge as if you were blind hemming a skirt or a pair of trousers.

2. Thread your machine with a good-quality monofilament or polyester invisible thread. For light fabrics, use the clear thread; for dark fabrics, use the smoke-colored thread. For the bobbin, use a neutral-color thread or one that matches the fabric color. For invisible appliqué, using a finer bobbin thread such as Bobbinfil (Mettler) or Bottom Line (Superior Threads) is preferable.

3. Use a size 60/8 or 70/10 needle. The 60/8 needles make a smaller hole and are the preferred option, but they are not always readily available. The monofilament thread is very fine, so it will fill only a small hole; hence the preference for finer needles. Take care though, because these needles are easily snapped in half if you pull your work too quickly out from under the needle.

4. Adjust your stitch width so that the stitch is just wide enough to barely catch two or three threads of the fabric. Adjust the stitch length so the zigzag stitches are ⅛″ (3mm) to ¼″ (7mm) apart. The exact settings will depend on the brand of your machine. When your stitch is invisible or almost invisible, then you have adjusted your machine correctly.

5. Adjust the top and bobbin tension as needed. Begin by reducing the top tension slightly, that is, turning your top tension dial to one number lower than normal. On the Bernina, thread the bobbin thread through the finger on the bobbin to tighten up the bobbin tension. On other machines you can tighten the bobbin tension as described on page 38.

6. To check your settings, make a sample with your fabrics on tear-away stabilizer. Press under the top edge ¼″ (7mm), and overlap the fabric. Pin the fabrics close to the folded edge as shown, placing the pins perpendicular to the fold.

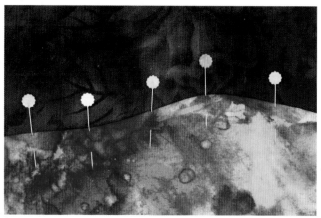
Sample ready to be stitched

7. Stitch along the edge of the fold with the straight stitches on the background fabric as close as possible to the folded edge of the top layer.

Only the zigzag stitch should bite into the top layer. If you see any of the bobbin thread coming through to the top, then you need to decrease your top tension further. If you have reduced your top tension all the way and can still see your bobbin thread on top, then tighten the bobbin tension. If you are using a finer bobbin thread than normal, then tightening your bobbin case before you start sewing is a good idea.

8. When you are happy with the invisible appliqué stitches on the practice sample, you are ready to sew your project. If necessary, change the bobbin thread to match your background fabric to ensure that the stitches will be invisible.

Blind hemming is almost invisible on patterned fabrics.

TIP

Although the blind hem stitch is standard on most machines, on a few machines you can't change the width of the stitch. If this is the case with your machine, you can still use the wider setting, but you'll need to run a line of quilting through the resulting line of needle holes, ¼″ (7mm) from the edge of your appliqué. Alternatively, you can use a very narrow zigzag stitch with clear monofilament thread. If you are in the market for a new sewing machine, find out whether you can change the settings on the machine you are considering because the invisible machine appliqué stitch is a useful and time-saving stitch to have in your repertoire.

Horizontal Satin Stitch

Horizontal satin stitch is my own name for a stitch that looks like satin stitch but is actually multiple rows of free-motion stitching on top of and next to one another. It is a useful stitch for appliquéing small pieces that look good with a solid edge or are prone to fraying. Satin stitching around a small shape without creating gaps is difficult, so just free-motion stitch a few times around each shape for a similar effect. Tie off the thread ends on the back of your work.

Horizontal satin stitch around small leaves

Programmed Stitches

Quite a few of the stitches that are programmed into your machine can be used for appliqué. Be adventurous and try some of these around the outside edges of your fused motifs. A stitch that I find effective both for appliqué and for stitching bold lines is the triple stitch. Most machines will have this stitch, which is made up of four stitches forward, two stitches back, four stitches forward, and so on. It effectively goes over each stitch three times, creating quite a strong line, especially if you use a 30-weight thread.

Triple stitch creates lattice on windmill vanes in **Vintage Wind Power** (page 75).

Embellishing and Quilting With Free-Motion Stitching

In addition to appliqué, free-motion stitching can be used to highlight details on leaves, to create rugged edges on rocks, to shade trees and foliage, to create reflections and shadows, and to add texture to various surfaces. The same techniques can be used for quilting, but the fabric stabilizer is not necessary when you are quilting the three layers together.

If you are new to free-motion stitching, read through the section on raw-edge appliqué earlier in this chapter, which details setting up your machine. Instead of stitching around the edge of a motif, it is now time to shade, draw, and create patterns, all the things you would normally do with a pencil or paint brush if you were a landscape artist.

Once again, practice on a sample before you launch into your masterpiece. Place some stabilizer under the area to be embellished and thread your machine. The top thread can be any weight from 20- to 50-weight. I prefer the 30- or 40-weight thread for most of my embellishing because it is easy to manage and is thick enough to build up quickly and be noticed. In the bobbin, you can choose one of the finer bobbin threads or use a thread that matches the top. (See page 36 for the appropriate needle type and size.)

Practice on sample backed with stabilizer.

There are numerous ways that you can hold your work to get as much control as possible as you free-motion stitch. I usually hold the work flat with my left hand on the top and move the fabric with my right hand holding on from underneath. Some quilters prefer to place both hands on the top of the work, and others use aids such as gloves with small rubber dots that assist in the manipulation of the fabric. Just as your machine stitching speed is a personal preference, you will also find that with practice, you develop your own comfortable position for holding your work as you move it under the needle.

Place the fabric backed with tear-away stabilizer under the darning foot. Lower the foot and then lower the needle into the work. Gradually move the fabric while stitching, trying to keep the stitches even. Without turning the fabric, stitch while moving it forward, backward, and sideways. Try small circles and spirals. The faster you move the fabric, the longer the stitches; the slower you move it, the shorter. It takes a while to get even stitches, but with practice you'll develop the ability to stitch in any direction and to create fluid lines. Secure the thread ends by tying them together on the back of your work.

Shade foliage using free-motion stitching techniques, as in **Tidal Images** (page 24).

If the stitching is to be quite intensive, stretching your work in a hoop may be helpful. Use a wooden embroidery hoop placed upside down (opposite the way you would normally use it for hand embroidery), so that the fabric is sitting flush on the sewing machine bed with the hoop above the work. You can easily hold onto the hoop and move it back and forth to build up the embroidery.

Free-Motion Quilting

If you are free-motion quilting, the correct tension setting is crucial. Both sides of your work will be on show, so you need to have balanced, even stitches on the top and the bottom. Test your stitches and threads on a sample that is made up of the fabrics and batting you plan to use. Practice stitching your sample the way you intend to quilt your project.

Free-Motion Zigzag Stitches

Try free-motion stitching on the zigzag setting. Vary your stitch width to create different effects. Usually, you will find that you have to loosen the top tension more than you do for straight free-motion stitching because the wider zigzag stitch creates more drag and puckers more easily.

Strappy leaves drawn with thread in **Tropical Seascape** (page 12).

Free-motion zigzag is great for shading foliage and filling in texture. You can change colors, overlapping the stitches, or try shading with a variegated thread for effective results. Try running off the edge of your fused shape onto the background to produce a textured edge.

Free-motion zigzag foliage in **African Thorn Tree** (page 84)

Try some of the following patterns and then make up some of your own.

Embellishing With Thicker Threads

Some threads are far too thick to pass through the needle and the tensioning plates on the top of the sewing machine. These threads can be easily wound onto a bobbin, either manually or using your bobbin-winding mechanism.

Of course, when you're using a decorative thread in the bobbin, the piece has to be sewn from the back. So that you know where to stitch, free-motion stitch an outline of the area to be embroidered from the top of your work using a finer thread in a similar shade. Use the settings as outlined above for this part of the process.

Before sewing with the thicker thread, check your bobbin tension. Pull out a short length of the bobbin thread from the bobbin case to make sure it slides out smoothly. Because you are using a thicker thread than normal, the tension will probably feel too tight. Loosen the screw on the bobbin case by turning it to the left about 10 minutes on the clock face. Recheck by pulling out more of the thread until you are happy that it glides out smoothly, without too much drag.

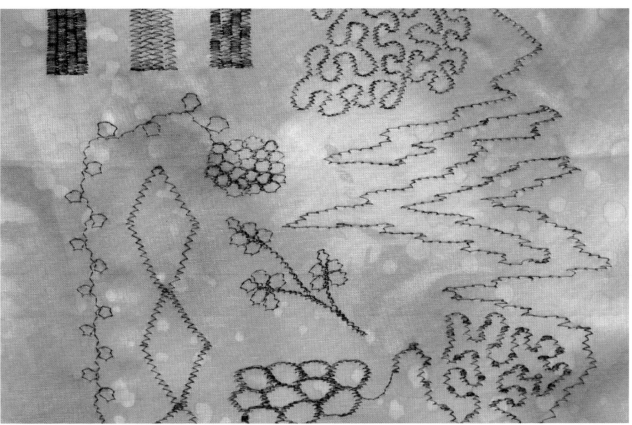

Free-motion zigzag patterns

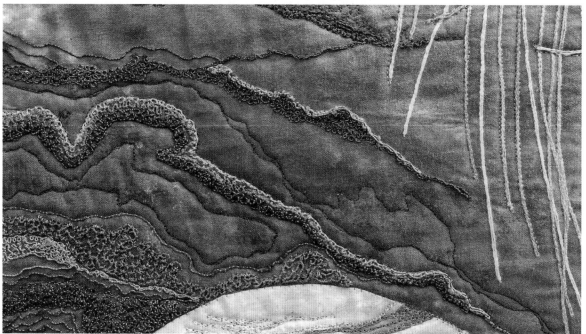

Create moss on rocks with thicker thread, as in **Grass Trees** (page 15).

If you enjoy stitching with thicker threads, purchasing another bobbin case to have permanently set on a looser setting is a good investment. Label this second bobbin case to distinguish it from your regular case. Some machines, especially those with a set-in bobbin case, allow you to bypass the bobbin tension altogether. Just place your bobbin in the bobbin case and then draw up the bobbin thread through the throat plate, ready to start stitching. Don't thread it through the narrow slot first; just leave it loose.

Insert the bobbin case containing the thicker thread into your machine, matching the shade of the bobbin thread with your finer top thread. Tighten the top tension to a higher setting than normal. You can also experiment using different colored threads on the top, and varying the top tension during stitching for interesting effects.

Free-motion stitch from the back of your work, creating closely stitched textures or free-flowing lines. I suggest that you use two layers of stabilizer, sew at a slower speed, and make the stitches a little larger to show off your beautiful threads. To finish off, take the thicker threads to the back of your work and tie them off with their buddies on the back. If you are using thicker threads for quilting, you must stitch them in by hand, or they will tend to unravel if you just cut them off.

Patterns using thicker threads

You can construct your landscape quilt in several different ways. You can appliqué, piece areas together, or fuse them to a background fabric. You will need to look at your design to decide which technique is the most appropriate. You may end up using all three of these techniques in one quilt. For all the techniques, you need to sketch your design (see pages 24–26), enlarge the sketch into a full-size pattern, construct the background, and then embellish the foreground details on the surface.

Contoured Landscape Construction

1. Make a full-size pattern of your design.

Once you are satisfied with your sketch, enlarge the background areas to the proposed finished size of your quilt. You can use a grid to scale up your sketch, or just redraw it to full size. Use a black marker to make the lines bold enough to allow them to be traced.

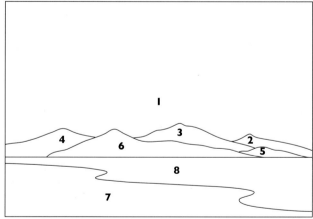
Draw your full-size pattern.

Going from a small sketch to a full-size drawing can make a big difference to the composition. Some areas may require additional detail, and some shapes that worked well in the small sketch may have to be redrawn. Make sure you are happy with the design before you go on. Changing the drawing now is much easier than changing it in the middle of quilt construction.

2. Determine the construction order for the background areas.

Divide the background into manageable areas. Concentrate on the larger background areas and ignore the details, which will be appliquéd or embroidered at a later time. Perhaps you can construct the sky and land areas separately and then join them later. Decide on a construction order for the background areas. Mark with arrows any edges that are to be turned under if you are appliquéing the areas together. When you are considering a background made of mountains and fields, the sky is applied first, then the most distant mountain, then the second most distant, and so on, gradually working your way forward.

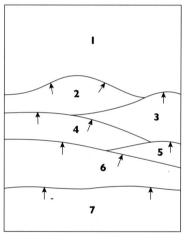
Number pieces from background to foreground. Mark edges to turn under.

If your design features a seascape, then you will probably place the sand in position first, with the waves overlapping the shore. Gradually add additional sea pieces, working your way out to the horizon.

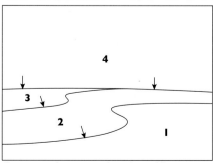
For water to lap over sand, apply sand first.

3. Trace the design on stabilizer and freezer paper.

Cut a piece of tear-away stabilizer slightly larger than your full-size pattern; allow a margin of approximately 2″ (5cm) around the design. There are different grades of tear-away stabilizer, so keep in mind that it needs to be firm enough to pin fabric to the surface without ripping but not so firm that it is difficult to tear away at the end of the process. Don't use iron-on stabilizer.

Trace the outline from your full size pattern onto the stabilizer. Replicate the original pattern and include the construction order numbers. Trace the design with a pencil or a ballpoint pen. Do not use a felt-tipped pen because some of the ink may transfer to your fabric at a later stage.

Repeat this process, tracing from the full-size pattern onto the paper side of the freezer paper (not the shiny side). On the freezer paper, mark the edges to be turned under with arrows and again include a number indicating the construction order of each area. You don't need to move the freezer paper to leave spaces between the pieces. Trace as a whole, replicating your original pattern. Cut out the individual freezer-paper patterns for each area.

4. Audition fabrics.

Use the original colored sketch as a guide to audition your fabrics for the first background area. Pin up your pieces of fabric on the wall over the area to be covered on the full-size drawing. Try fabrics with different textures and patterns, and experiment with different color combinations, keeping in mind the illusion of depth or contrast you are trying to create. Step back and see how the fabrics work from a distance. Try squinting or use a reducing glass to see whether you have created the desired effect.

Audition your fabrics.

5. Cut out the fabrics.

Place the appropriate freezer-paper pattern on the right side of your selected fabric, making sure there is at least ½″ (1.3cm) of fabric around the edges of the pattern. Iron the freezer-paper pattern, shiny side down, onto the fabric. Cut out the fabric with a ½″ (1.3cm) seam allowance around all the edges.

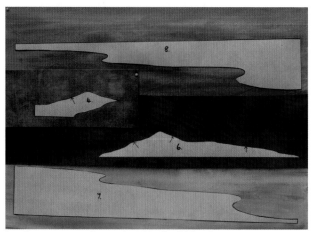
Iron freezer-paper pattern onto right side of fabric.

Trim the edge that is to be turned under to ¼″ (7mm). This edge is marked with an arrow. Clip curves where necessary to allow the seam allowance to lie flat.

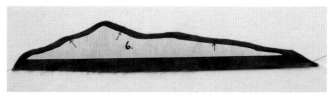
Trim edge marked with arrow to ¼″ (7mm).

Fold the ¼″ (7mm) seam allowance to the back of the piece and press.

Press seam allowance to back.

Front view of piece

TIP

I find that if I place the freezer-paper side of the piece down on the ironing board and pull back the seam allowance until I can just see the edge of the freezer paper, I can get a neatly pressed-under edge. If the piece is really curved, a line of stay stitching just out from the edge of the freezer-paper pattern will help to produce effortless curves. Ensure that your stay stitching will disappear under the edge by placing it about 1/16″ (2mm) away from the freezer-paper pattern.

6. Position the pieces on tear-away stabilizer.

With the freezer paper still attached, place the sky piece on the stabilizer, matching the edges of the piece with the lines drawn on the stabilizer. Pin the piece in position.

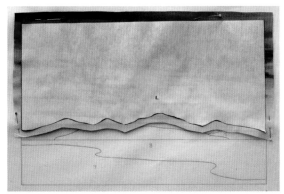

Place sky in position using pattern drawn on stabilizer as guide.

With the freezer paper still attached, place the next piece in the correct position on the stabilizer, overlapping the adjacent fabric. Pin the second piece in place with a minimum of pins and then carefully remove the freezer paper. Pin again every 2″ (5cm), placing the pins at right angles to the curved, pressed-under edge of the piece.

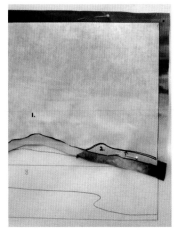

Match up freezer-paper pattern with lines on stabilizer.

Pin every 2″ (5cm), placing pins at right angles to edge.

Repeat this process with the next adjacent area until the whole background is covered. It is now time to stand back and view your quilt from a distance once again. Check that you have created the illusion of depth as seen in your original photo or sketch. When you are working at an arm's length, it is easy to get absorbed in your design and color selection and then miss what happens when you stand back.

7. Attach the pieces using invisible machine appliqué.

When you are happy with your fabric selection and placement, sew the pieces in order to the tear-away stabilizer using invisible machine appliqué (see pages 45–46).

Stitch piece in place using invisible machine appliqué.

All pieces stitched in place

8. Appliqué and embroider.

Once the background is stitched to the stabilizer, it is time to add the surface details. Refer back to your original sketch and carefully draw these features on your full-size pattern. Areas of land or water that were too narrow or fine to be part of the background construction can be fused on the background. You can add trees, buildings, rocks, animals, and so on using either raw-edge, satin-stitch, or hand appliqué. Note that as you add the appliqué and embroidery, the stabilizer will help to stabilize the work for intensive stitching.

9. Remove the tear-away stabilizer.

When the surface is completed, gently remove as much of the tear-away stabilizer from the back as possible. Tweezers or small scissors will assist in those tricky corners.

Mosaic Landscape Construction

You may decide that some areas of your landscape would look more effective if constructed using a simple mosaic technique.

Follow Steps 1, 2, and 3 as outlined for the contoured landscape construction process (pages 51–52) and then choose areas to be constructed by the mosaic technique. This technique involves the piecing together of lots of small shapes to make up a larger area. You can use squares, diamonds, rectangles, or irregular shapes joined together to make one piece of fabric. This method works well where variation in texture and color is required, such as for vegetation, the sea, and so on. You can also use this technique to create an interesting pieced sky.

1. Choose the square sizes.

Decide on the size of squares for the construction of your background, taking into account the overall size of your finished quilt. For a quilt that is larger than 30″ (76cm) on one side, 2″ (5cm) squares are appropriate. If the quilt is to be smaller, then the square size can be reduced to 1¾″ (4.5cm) or 1½″ (4cm). Squares that are smaller than this take a long time to piece, but using small squares may be worth the effort if you want to incorporate many different fabrics for a special effect.

You aren't limited to using squares of only one size. The size can be varied for different areas as long as the sizes of squares in adjoining areas are multiples of each other.

Examples:
2″, 4″, 8″ (cut 2½″, 4½″, 8½″)
5cm, 10cm, 20cm (cut 6.3cm, 11.3cm, 21.3cm)

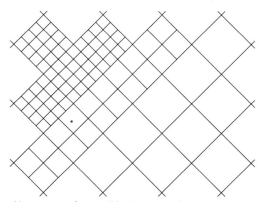

Use squares of compatible sizes to match seams.

By using these sizes, you can join squares of various sizes together with matching seams. If the mosaic areas are not adjacent, the sizes of the squares can vary without causing distraction.

2. Draw a grid.

Use your chosen measurements to draw a grid on both the freezer paper and the stabilizer. To draw the grid, place the 45° line of a gridded ruler on the edge of the freezer paper. Draw a diagonal line. Continue drawing lines as far apart as the finished size of the squares. To complete the squares, place a vertical line on your ruler on one of the original lines, and draw additional lines at right angles to the original lines. Trace over these lines onto your tear-away stabilizer. Trace using a ruler to ensure accuracy.

For a mosaic sky, just draw the grid on the stabilizer.

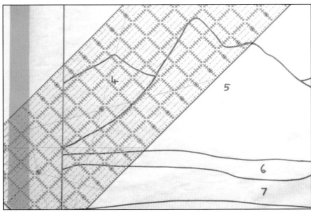

Draw lines on freezer paper using 45° line on ruler.

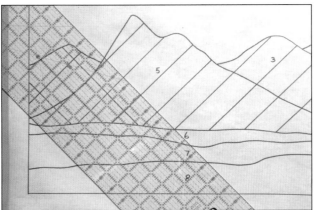

Draw second group of lines at right angles to first.

Cut out your squares of fabric, remembering to add ½″ (1.3cm) for seam allowances. Stack the squares in color groups.

3. Arrange the squares on the stabilizer.

Place the squares on point to soften the edges and to allow smoother blending. Work on one area at a time but keep adjacent areas of the quilt in mind. To assist in the creation of perspective and depth, place the larger squares in the foreground, graduating to the smallest squares in the distant background. The squares drawn on the stabilizer are the finished size, so you will need to overlap the edges of the fabric squares to get them to fit. Rather than placing the squares randomly, arrange them in groups of color and texture. Groups of 3 or 5 usually help create the illusion of variations in foliage, whereas totally random placement can lead to confusion and a lack of definition.

Arrange squares on tear-away stabilizer.

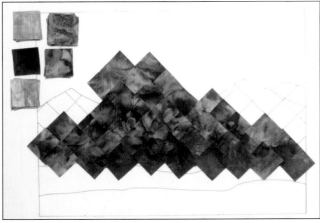

Squares will overlap lines.

Half-square triangles can also be used for special effects. To save cutting 2 larger triangles, just place 2 squares on top of each other and sew from corner to corner. Trim to create a ¼″ (7mm) seam allowance on the back.

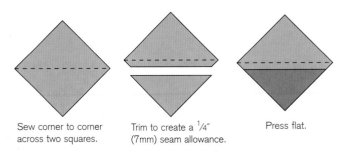

Sew corner to corner across two squares.

Trim to create a ¼″ (7mm) seam allowance.

Press flat.

Assemble each area, making sure you have enough pieces to completely cover each shape.

4. Sew the squares together.

When you are happy with the placement, sew your squares together with an accurate ¼″ (7mm) seam. First sew the squares into diagonal rows.

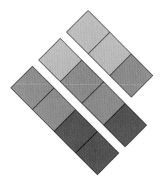

Join squares in diagonal rows.

Press the seam allowances for each row in alternate directions. Nest the seams and pin the first 2 rows together at the opposing seam allowances.

Sew the rows together with an accurate ¼″ (7mm) seam allowance. Press these new seams all in the same direction. These joined pieces are then treated as one piece of fabric.

5. Cut out the pieces.

Press the freezer-paper pattern, shiny side down, onto the top of your pieced fabric in its correct place, matching the grid with your seamlines.

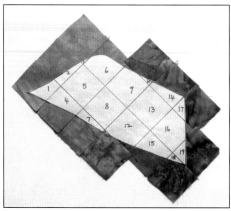

Match grid lines with seamlines.

Cut pieces with ½″ (1.3cm) seam allowances around all the edges of the freezer paper. Trim the edges to be turned under to ¼″ (7mm), clipping curves where necessary.

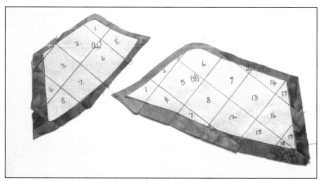

Trim edges to be stitched.

Press the ¼″ (7mm) seam allowance to the back using the freezer-paper edge as a guide.

6. Position the pieces on tear-away stabilizer.

With the freezer paper still attached, place the pieces in the correct positions on the stabilizer, overlapping adjacent seam allowances, and pin the pieces in place. Place pins at right angles to the curved, pressed-under edges of the pieces.

Pin in correct position.

Repeat this process with the next adjacent area until all the pieces are added. When you are happy with your fabric selection and placement, attach each piece to the stabilizer in the correct order, using invisible machine appliqué. (Refer to Steps 8 and 9 on page 54 to continue the construction.)

Attach each piece in order.

Make sure seamlines match.

All pieces in place

Fused Landscape Construction

An alternative method that is effective for small landscapes is to fuse the fabric pieces, except the sky, to a foundation of stabilizer. This method is similar to the contoured landscape technique, but instead of turning under the top edge of each piece to appliqué it in position, you cut the top edge to the finished size and fuse the piece in position. The lower edges have a seam allowance that extends under the edge of the adjacent fused piece. The pieces are then held in place with free-motion stitching.

1. Make a full-size pattern of your design and determine construction order.

Follow Steps 1 and 2 as outlined for the contoured landscape construction process (page 51) to make a full-size pattern of the design and determine the construction order of the background areas.

2. Trace the design on stabilizer and trace the sky onto freezer paper.

3. Trace the design on fusible web.

Use the reverse image of your pattern to trace all the pattern pieces except the sky onto the paper side of the fusible web. On the fusible web, mark the number of each piece and draw the ¼″ (7mm) seam allowances for the edges that will tuck under the adjacent pieces. I draw dashed lines for the seam allowances. You will also need to add seam allowances to all edges that meet the borders. Move the fusible web after tracing each piece to leave ½″ (1.3cm) of space between each subsequent piece. Cut out the individual fusible web pieces, allowing a ¼″ (7mm) margin around each shape. Remember that these fusible web shapes will be mirror images of the original shapes.

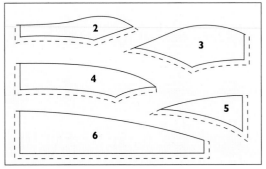

Add seam allowances to edges that tuck under adjacent pieces.

For seascapes, the edge of the wave nearest the shoreline would be cut on the drawn line, and the sand and the horizon side of the wave would have seam allowances to tuck under the next wave.

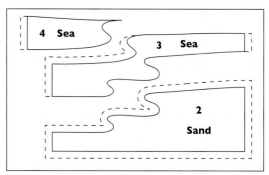

Leave space between pieces. Add seam allowances to edges that tuck under adjacent pieces.

4. Audition fabrics.

Audition your fabrics for the sky and background areas, trying fabrics in different colors and textures.

Audition fabrics for sky and background.

5. Cut out the fabrics.

Sky

Press the freezer-paper pattern onto the right side of your selected sky fabric. Cut out the sky, leaving ½″ (1.3cm) seam allowances around the edge. Position this piece on the stabilizer, lining up the edge of your freezer-paper patterns with the traced outline on the stabilizer. Note that the sky area will not be fused but will instead be held in place by the borders or bindings, the top of the hills, and other pieces.

Iron freezer-paper pattern onto sky fabric.

Other Background Pieces

Place the fusible web shapes on the back of the selected fabrics, making sure that there is at least ½″ (1.3cm) of fabric around each shape. Press the fusible web, rough side down, onto the fabric. Cut out the fabric on the lines drawn on the fusible web. Remember to include the seam allowances to tuck under adjacent shapes.

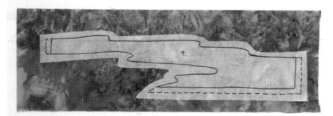

Press fusible web onto back of selected fabric.

Remove the fusible web paper and place each piece in the correct position on the stabilizer, overlapping the adjacent seam allowances, and then pin the pieces in place. For accurate placement, use the traced pattern on the stabilizer as a guide.

Place piece in correct position, overlapping adjacent seam allowances.

All background pieces in position

Repeat this process with the next adjacent area until a large area or even the whole background is filled in.

Stand back and view your quilt to check whether you have created the illusion of depth as seen in your original photo or sketch.

If you are happy with your fabric choices, fuse the fabrics in place, following the fusible web manufacturer's instructions.

6. Stitch down the pieces using raw-edge appliqué.

Stitch around each piece, using free-motion stitching. (This technique is outlined on page 43.) If your pieces are fairly straight or only slightly curved, you might feel more comfortable using a straight stitch with the feed dogs up.

7. Appliqué and embroider.

Refer back to your original sketch or photo and draw the surface details on your full-size pattern. Add trees, buildings, people, and so on, using either raw-edge, satin-stitch, or hand appliqué. Add grasses and extra foliage using free-motion machine embroidery techniques (see pages 47–50). Depending on your design, sandwiching and quilting the background before adding trees and other embroidery may be easier.

8. Remove the stabilizer.

Before quilting, remove the tear-away stabilizer behind the sky piece. The rest of the stabilizer can be left in position.

trees

I love trees. I love their shapes, their smells, their textures, the wonderful colors of their bark, the play of light on their foliage, the whisper of the wind rustling through their leaves. Trees can be stately and beautiful or ugly and grotesque. They can be tall and majestic, fine and slender, or twisted and tortured. They can be masculine or feminine. Although they have an identifiable pattern to their foliage, they have a character of their own.

Trees are probably the most dominant element that landscape artists feature in their work. Trees provide us with an enormous variety of colors and forms, so build up your own collection of sketches and photos for a never-ending source of inspiration.

Each tree is like a piece of sculpture, and their wonderful silhouettes look stunning when juxtaposed against a beautiful sunset sky. Even if your tree photos were not taken at sunset, they can be a valuable resource for drawing trees for your designs.

As you read through this chapter, you'll find that much of the theory covered in the chapters on color and stitching techniques is applied in a practical way to trees. In the same way, the techniques covered in this chapter can be used to fashion other elements besides trees.

Compose Your Design

When you are composing, don't hesitate to move nature around. You can eliminate, move around, or add trees, making sure that they fit naturally into your design. Anchoring trees to the ground is crucial. Trees do not sit on top of the ground but extend upward from a vast root system beneath the surface. If your tree is growing in a grassy area, show some of the grass hiding part of the trunk. Including the exposed roots of a tree can be interesting because of the varied shapes and the wonderful diagonal angles they can create in your work.

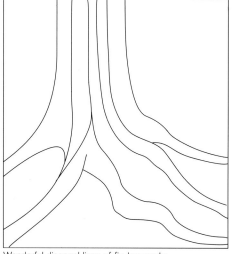
Wonderful diagonal lines of fig tree roots

Grass hiding part of exposed roots

Twin boab trees   Fascinating variations in texture   Trees are wonderful sources of inspiration.

Rearrange any limbs that take your eye out of the picture. By changing the direction of some of the major branches, you can improve the movement and vitality of your work and keep the viewer interested.

and trunks accordingly. When foliage is seen from a distance, the textures are minimal. Nearly flat, greenish shapes can be used to depict trees on far-away hillsides. The focus should be on the colors and unified shapes rather than on the details of single trees or bushes. In a close-up view, however, you should look for characteristic textures to represent specific trees.

Linking or overlapping trees can also bring harmony to your work as well as enhancing perspective. Rather than having trees spaced at equal intervals standing stiff and tall like soldiers, try overlapping two trees and placing a third a short distance away. Trees are also one of the major links between the earth and sky. A tree can provide that important link to join the foreground and background, crossing through the horizon.

Rearrange limbs that lead straight out of picture.

Creating Perspective With Trees

Conveying depth in your landscape is important, and trees are a useful element for this purpose. Remember that trees get smaller as they recede into the distance. To give your work a feeling of deep space, place large, detailed tree shapes in the front and gradually diminish the sizes and detail of the trees as they recede. Remember that colors fade as objects move into the distance, so change the color of your foliage

Overlapping links elements.

Dramatic silhouettes   Tree roots clinging to riverbank   Trees can link foreground with background.

Be aware of the position of the sun when you are shading in the colors on the trunk, branches, and foliage. Create wonderful contrast of lights and darks by taking advantage of where the sun's rays kiss your trees. The surfaces facing the sun will reflect the beautiful colors of your sunset sky while those further away will be dark and in shadow. As the light changes quickly, use your camera to record the effect the light has on different areas of the landscape. From your photos, study the effects of reflected light on the trunk and shadow sides of the branches.

Note pink glow reflected on side of branches.

Tips for Drawing Trees

When you create a tree, you need to simplify the image, making many decisions along the way. You will be using lots of pieces of information, which when joined together will inform your viewer of the type of tree. Knowledge of the main characteristics of shape, trunks, branches, and leaves is important, and you may need to research your species of trees to become familiar with its main features.

Consider the pattern of the branches. See how they taper; check whether the trunk divides lower down or toward the top of the tree. Trunks usually taper toward the top, and branches grow up and away from the main trunk. Imagine that you are at a life-drawing class and try drawing the tree without its covering of foliage. Studies of dead trees also help us to understand their structure. By continually drawing trees, you will certainly develop your skills.

Poplar tree

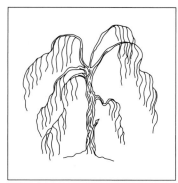
Willow tree

Norfolk palm tree

Gum tree

Now look at the foliage. The outline and density of the canopy are of critical importance. Sometimes the outline is clear and solid; at other times there is just a vague sprinkling of leaves across the sky. Eucalyptus trees are characterized by the delicacy of their foliage, in contrast to the maple's rich green canopy that almost hides the sky completely. You cannot add details of every leaf on a tree, but by building up a general background of the canopy, you can add suggestions of leaf details at the end. Think about the edges and make them interesting and full of character.

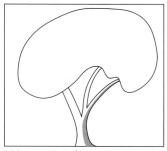

Add suggestion of leaves to make edges full of character.

Leaves come in an incredible variety of textures, sizes, shapes, and colors, and you must select a technique that allows you to capture these differences. Sponging or dry brushing with paint, fusing small pieces of fabric, and stippling or coloring with thread are all useful techniques that can be used in combination or alone. The important thing is to simplify the foliage while taking into account its distinctive shape, size, and color.

Thorn tree in South Africa has dense foliage and distinctive shape.

In contrast, casuarina foliage is light and delicate.

Creating Trees

Draw your trees on your original pattern. After considering the shapes of the trunks and foliage, decide on the methods you will use to create these trees on your background.

Technique 1: Fusible Appliqué

Probably the simplest and easiest approach is to cut out the trunk and foliage from fabric, fuse them in place, and then stitch around the edges. This technique works well for simple shapes where the foliage is well defined and the trunk is not too fine. This process involves the use of fusible web (see pages 39–40).

Trunk

With a pencil, trace the trunk and branches onto a piece of fusible web. Remember that you will get a mirror image unless you reverse the original drawing using a lightbox or window. Cut out the shape, leaving about ¼″ (7mm) around the outside of your pencil outline. Select your fabric and use a hot, dry iron to press the fusible web onto the back of the fabric. Cut out the shape on the line. Peel off the backing paper, position the trunk on the background, and iron it in place.

Position trunk and iron it in place.

It is now time to stitch the trunk to your background. There are many ways you can do this, but I recommend free-motion stitching. Using this technique, you can stitch in any direction, making it easier to go around branches that head off in all directions. (See pages 47–49 for detailed information on free-motion stitching.) Remember to place a piece of tear-away stabilizer under your work before stitching. The stabilizer helps to keep the work flat and provides a firm surface to work on.

Foliage

Choose a fabric that allows a variation of light and dark shades. Hand-dyed fabrics with their variations of color and value are especially useful for foliage. Fuse a square of fabric to fusible web. Keep the shape of the foliage in mind as you cut out some shapes that can be overlapped to create your tree. Try cutting free-hand so you can take advantage of the variations in color. If you are not comfortable with this process, you can trace some shapes from your original drawing onto the fusible web before ironing it onto the back of your fabric.

Fuse foliage in position and then stitch.

Alternatively, trace the shapes onto freezer paper, cut them out, and iron them onto the right side of the fabric backed with fusible web. Cut out the fabric shapes using the freezer-paper outline as a guide. Remove the backing paper and place the tree shapes on your background.

Cut out shapes, taking advantage of color variations.

Overlap foliage shapes, leaving sky holes.

Trace foliage shapes onto freezer paper and press onto prepared fabric.

Cut out shapes, using freezer paper as guide.

Position shapes on background and press in place.

Try various arrangements of foliage until you are happy that your tree has the same characteristics as your original. Cut many small pieces rather than fewer larger pieces. Remember to leave sky holes, that is, places where the sky is visible through your trees. When you are happy with the arrangement, press it with a hot iron to fuse the shapes to the background. Free-motion stitch the tree in place with matching thread using either a straight or zigzag stitch.

Dead Trees

This method of fusing fabric is also ideal for creating dead trees. Trace your trunk and branches onto a piece of fusible web. Look at the edges of the original and carefully replicate the roughness, the broken limbs, and the lumps and bumps. Give your tree character.

Replicate character of dead tree branches.

For some dead trees, free-motion stitching extra branches may be appropriate. You can draw these extra branches using your preferred marking pen and then stitch over the drawn lines three or four times to get enough width and depth. Alternatively, keep your original sketch in mind and just stitch the branches in without marking them first. Add more fine branches until you have the effect you are after, being careful not to overdo it.

Free-motion stitch extra branches.

Technique 2: Embroidered Trunk and Foliage

Your tree may lend itself to being embroidered in thread. Transferring the image to the right side through multiple layers of fabric can be quite difficult, especially when the background has been pieced. The following simple technique allows you to accurately transfer a pattern to your quilt top without using a lightbox or guesswork.

Trace the tree outline onto a piece of tear-away stabilizer. Tracing will result in a mirror image, so outline the shape on the reverse side of the stabilizer and use this side as your guide. Before transferring your pattern to the back of the stabilizer, label the right side to avoid confusion.

Tree outline ready to trace onto tear-away stabilizer

Pin tear-away guide to back of quilt top.

Pin this guide in position on the back of your quilt top. Thread your machine with the desired thread and matching bobbin thread. The bobbin thread will appear on the right side of your work, so you need to choose a color that will blend well with the embroidered foliage. A wise choice for the mangrove tree in the photo was a medium shade of purple. The bobbin thread color must be bold enough to be seen, yet subtle enough to blend in.

Attach the darning foot and drop or cover the feed dogs. Adjust the stitch length and width to 0.

Because you are sewing from the reverse side of the fabric, you need to tighten the top tension. If your normal sewing tension is 5, try tension 7, 8, or even 9 on a practice sample to determine which setting gives the best stitch underneath your work, which is in fact the right side.

Stitch outline through to right side, following guide on tear-away stabilizer.

Place your work with the drawing of the tree on the stabilizer facing up under the darning foot, and then lower the presser foot. At this stage, your quilt top is right side down. Free-motion stitch along the outline of the tree, so that the image is transferred to the right side.

Now place the work right side up under the machine. Change the top tension back to a lower setting. If your usual tension setting is 5, then turn the tension to 3. Once again try different tension settings on your practice sample. When you are happy with the stitch, gradually shade in the tree shape with free-

Shade in tree outline with free-motion stitching.

motion embroidery stitches. Begin with the trunk, moving the fabric forward and backward, just as you would if shading with a pencil. Remember that the faster the work is moved, the longer the stitches will be, and the slower the movement, the shorter the stitches. It may be advisable to have your work stretched out in an embroidery hoop for this step.

Once the trunk is filled in, turn your work sideways and fill in the foliage using a similar forward and backward motion, working horizontally across the quilt surface. This is much easier on your shoulders and neck, but remember to give your self a break every 15 minutes to stretch.

Leave some open areas for sky holes, as in Tidal Images (page 24).

Vary the color of the top thread to give the illusion of light falling on the leaves. The thicker, 30-weight thread will fill in more quickly than the 40-weight. A combination of several weights of threads is quite acceptable and makes some areas appear slightly raised. Leave some areas open, so that the sky or background is visible through the foliage. Secure the thread ends by taking them through to the back and tying them off.

If your embroidery threatens to pucker, press the work with a medium-hot iron, using plenty of steam to flatten out any wayward bumps or gathers. A second piece of fabric stabilizer placed underneath can also assist in creating a firmer working surface.

Machine embroidery is also useful for creating smaller trees or other plants that are too delicate to be cut out of fabric. Distant tree lines made up of straggling trees or clumps of grass or ferns can be realistically stitched in thread. If you are game, you can stitch directly on your quilt top. Otherwise, follow the method just outlined to reproduce recognizable shapes.

Create smaller trees in thread.

Technique 3: Combination of Fusing and Machine Embroidery

Some trees lend themselves to having a fused fabric trunk and branches, but the foliage is too fine to be created in fabric. The pandanus palm is a good example. It has a beautiful, strong, curved trunk that allows you plenty of scope to enhance the design, but the foliage would be far too heavy if made of fabric. A combination of fusing and stitching is ideal for this tree and many others.

Pandanus palm

Fuse trunk in position and then stitch.

Fuse the trunk in position using the techniques outlined on pages 39–40. Carefully free-motion stitch around the edges of the tree trunk. Stitching around the trunk is much easier now rather than later, when the foliage has been added.

Now stitch your foliage. Look at your sketch, noting the thickness, direction, and texture of the foliage. Replicate these features in thread using free-motion stitching. If you don't feel confident to just launch into it, draw some guidelines to help get you started. After stitching a few clumps, you will probably feel confident to continue the process without any guidelines.

Outline area to be stitched and then fill in.

Another pandanus palm in different color scheme

Other trees have dense clumps of foliage that can be easily replicated in fabric, but the trunks are so fine that they need to be stitched. The distinctive mallee gum tree has almost ball-like clumps of foliage and numerous fine trunks.

Mallee gum tree

Original drawing

Once again, the trunk is stitched first, and then the foliage is added. Use a bold pencil or fine pen to trace the tree trunks from your original drawings onto a piece of tear-away stabilizer. Turn it over and transfer the drawing to the reverse side.

Pin the stabilizer to the reverse side of your pieced background and use free-motion stitching to stitch over the lines, remembering to increase your top tension.

Stitch from reverse side over lines drawn on tear-away stabilizer.

The bobbin thread is the one that will be visible, so make sure that the color of your bobbin thread matches the color you will use for your trunks. The outline of the trunks should now be visible on the right side of your work, and you can proceed to color them in further with thread.

Outline is visible on front.

Thicken lines further with thread.

Fuse the foliage in position and free-motion stitch around the edges in a matching thread.

Add foliage and stitch in place.

Technique 4: Fused Fabric Covered by Embroidery

For some trees, the amount of stitching needed to give a solid cover would be out of the question. Another technique that provides a base of color involves fusing the basic shapes to your quilt top and then shading over them with thread in the appropriate texture and color. By stitching over the edges onto the background fabric, you can make the edges much more textured and interesting, yet a huge buildup of thread is not necessary to get coverage.

Palm fronds with textured edges

Fuse the tree trunk and fronds using the methods outlined previously.

Use free-motion stitching to sew around the edge of your trunks and then begin to shade in the foliage. Continue stitching over the edges to give a more detailed outline. Try to replicate the textures and sweeping lines of the foliage as you stitch.

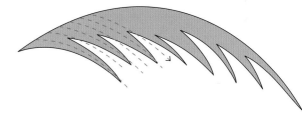

Stitch over edge onto background.

Fine texture on edges can be achieved.　　Fringed foliage is effective in silhouette.

Technique 5: Combinations of Fused Fabric, Stitching, and Painting

Some trees have a fine layer of foliage. To create this effect, and allow the sky to be quite visible through the leaves, try sponging or brushing the tree canopy using fabric paint. This technique is especially effective when you are working on a silhouette of trees in front of a glorious sunset sky.

Fuse and stitch the trunks and branches using the methods already outlined.

Fuse and stitch trunks.

Now revisit the initial photographs and drawings of your trees. Which direction does the foliage run? Is it more vertical and drooping like the foliage of the casuarina or willow, or is it more horizontal like that of many conifers? Is the canopy so thick that it hides the trunk and branches in places, or is it so sparse that the sky holes are quite evident? Does the canopy appear as clumps, or is it more evenly distributed? The answers to these questions will guide you as you decide on the techniques and equipment to use when applying your paint.

Sponge Paint Foliage for Light Covering of Foliage

Cut a piece of freezer paper slightly larger than the area to be painted. Press the freezer paper to the back of your fabric to give you a stable working surface. Pour some undiluted paint onto your palette or a saucer. Using multiple colors is most effective, so pour a little of each of several colors next to one another on your palette. For maximum control when painting, don't wet your background fabric. Use a sponge to pick up some paint and then dab off the excess onto a practice sample. You can control the amount of paint you apply with each dab. By allowing the sponge to absorb plenty of color, you can achieve a fairly dense covering. Alternately, the sponge can be squeezed gently until it is almost dry. When you are happy with the amount of paint being applied, begin to dab paint onto the trunks and branches. Remember that it will be darker in some areas than others. Give the foliage a shape that is not too symmetrical but shows some individuality. Be aware of the tops of the trees that receive the most light and have the finer branches. Do not create hard edges. Keep them soft by gently sponging on the paint.

Canopy appears as clumps with sky holes.

This technique is also useful for building up masses of background foliage. Draw the trunks with paint or thread, using irregular spacing and adding to or eliminating from your original drawing if necessary. Vary the heights of the foliage, making some areas wider, some thinner. You are really creating a pattern of lights and darks, with some areas denser than others. Look for the shapes of the trees silhouetted against each other. Place some of the trunks a little farther forward, away from the background mass to enhance the impression of depth.

Sponge background trees.

Sponge paint onto dry background to create light foliage.

Trees in background will be lighter.

Brush Paint Foliage for Direction and Substance

Brushes of various shapes and prices are available on the market. On most occasions, you do not need the more expensive brushes, and even an old shaving brush or stenciling brush can be useful for painting foliage. Fuse or stitch the trunks and branches in position and then apply the paint to the dry fabric, backed with freezer paper. Experiment with both a wet brush and a dry brush. To use a dry brush, load the brush with paint and wipe off excess moisture before making the marks on your fabric. A fairly stiff brush is often more useful for this technique.

A fan brush can also help you create interesting effects. Load the brush with paint and then work in a circular motion.

Paint Tree Trunks

Sometimes it is impossible to find the perfect fabric for tree trunks. A simple solution is to paint the trunks on white cotton fabric creating wonderful variations in color, value, and texture.

Trace or draw the outline of the trunk onto your fabric in pen or pencil. Iron a piece of freezer paper that is slightly larger than your tree onto the back of the fabric. Look at your original photo and paint in the lighter areas first. Gradually add more color, building up the layers of paint and texture.

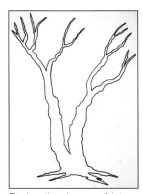

Trunk outline drawn on fabric

Add lots of different colors.

When the fabric is dry, iron it to set the paint. Iron a piece of fusible web onto the back of your fabric and then cut out your tree. You should be able to see your original drawn lines when the paint is dry. Remove the backing paper and press the trunk into position on your quilt top.

Cut out and fuse in place.

Trunk painted darker at top against sky

Fuse and stitch trunks.

Canopy created with stenciling brush

Fan brush used in different directions

Stitch Trunks and Foliage

Painted foliage and trunks can be further enhanced with stitching. Choose a stitching pattern that complements the original texture of the foliage, as I did in *Grass Trees* (page 15). This stitching can be done as part of the quilting process, or if the stitching is heavy, this embellishing can be completed before the quilt is sandwiched.

Painted background trees are enhanced with stitching.

Dense thread work is completed before sandwiching.

Trees With a Distinctive Shape or Character

There are some amazing trees that really stand out from the crowd, or should that be the forest? Their unique trunk shape or distinctive foliage provides wonderful inspiration, especially when they are presented as a strong image in silhouette form against a stunning sunset sky. Trees that just deserve to be noticed include the boab and grass trees in Australia, the Joshua tree in the deserts of the United States, the thorn trees from Africa, and many types of cactus, to name just a few. These wonderful creations can be portrayed in combinations of fabric, thread, and paint. They can be reproduced in accurate detail, or their strong shapes can be portrayed in a more abstract style.

Prickly giant cacti have real character.

Detail from **Kimberley Mystique** (page 6)

Joshua tree

Yuccas make a great silhouette.

I hope in this chapter I have conveyed to you my strong feelings for trees. I love to photograph them and draw them, and I am continually challenged to reproduce their textures and form in fabric and thread. Enjoy the adventure of collecting your own tree photos and drawings. They are certainly a never-ending source of inspiration.

other elements

There are many other elements such as grass, rocks, buildings, people, and reflections that you might want to include in your design. They may be the main feature or perhaps a supporting character. Whatever their role, you need to know their characteristics and structure to successfully integrate them into your landscape.

Grass

Grass tends to grow in all directions. It varies in height, width, and color. Some blades are straight and others curved.

Use grass to create interest and movement in your work. Grass blowing over in the wind suggests energy and can provide directional movement in your design. Grass growing around the roots of trees and at the base of rocks or buildings can soften hard edges and make structures look like they belong in the composition. In the same way, reeds and weeds can hide the edge of a lake or pond and break up long edges. Clumps of grass can also provide a link between areas as they overlap.

Some blades of grass are straight and others curved.

Clumps of grass can connect areas.

Individual blades of grass will be discernable only in the foreground. As the grass proceeds into the middle ground, it will appear smaller and the details will be blurred.

Grass can be created in paint or thread or a combination of the two. You can use very fine brushstrokes to lay down a background that gives intensity, and then add highlights in stitching. Vary the thickness of the threads for more definition and diversity.

Free-motion stitching is the easiest technique to use when creating grass because you have the liberating freedom to stitch in any direction.

Grass can be created in paint and stitching.

Rocks

Rocks, with their variations in texture, color, and shape, are a fascinating source of inspiration for artists. Rocks are full of folds, creases, and cracks, and their colors glow as the sun gracefully sets in the evening.

Bottom edges tend to be fairly horizontal.

Rocks are wonderful sources of inspiration.

Make sure that your rocks are firmly anchored to the ground or under the water and are not sitting on top. Often more than half the rock is under the surface, so the bottom edges tend to be fairly flat rather than rounded. If you work at making sure there are areas of shadows in your rock surfaces, their dimension will come automatically. It is important to get the outside shape right and then go back and add details.

Rock shapes are defined by sunlight and shadows.

Fabric painted in colors to harmonize with landscape

There are many commercial fabrics on the market that replicate rocks. These fabrics can be used in moderation in the foreground of your design. Often the color is not in harmony with the rest of your landscape, so feel free to paint over the pattern with a transparent paint to get the desired effect. You may be able to fussy cut around some of the rocks and then overlap them to get a natural composition.

Fussy cut around edges of individual rocks.

Another alternative is to paint rocks on white fabric backed with freezer paper. Draw the outline of the rocks in pen or pencil and then shade them in with paint. Indentations and shading of darker areas will give the rocks shape and form. Use brushstrokes to create curved surfaces.

Rocks can be hand painted on plain fabric and then cut out and fused in place.

Rocks are often covered with intriguing areas of colorful lichen. These fascinating textures can be replicated in closely stitched areas of free-motion embroidery using thicker thread. (See pages 49–50 for advice on these techniques.)

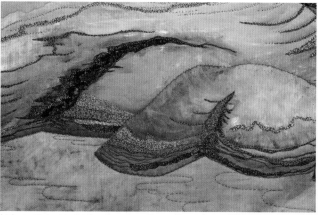

Lichen stitched in thicker thread on Grass Trees (page 15)

Man-Made Structures

Many familiar man-made structures can work effectively as silhouettes when juxtaposed against a sunset sky. The secret is to keep the shapes simple by picking out the main features that make the structures arresting and eye-catching, but also identifiable, in silhouette.

Choose structures that are appealing and full of character. Shapes that are simple but strong, such as fence posts, windmills, silos, derelict barns, and so on, work well as silhouettes.

Old water tanks would look wonderful positioned against sunset sky.

Windmill—an Australian icon

Vintage Wind Power,
15.75″ × 21.5″
(40cm × 55cm),
Gloria Loughman

Draw the outline of the structure on your pattern, making sure the size and perspective are in keeping with your design. Trace the outline through to the back of your pattern using a lightbox or a window. Trace this outline onto fusible web and iron the web to the back of your selected fabric. When shapes require more than one fabric, extend the edge to tuck under the adjacent shape.

Fuse the shapes to the background and stitch around the edge of the shapes with either a straight or satin stitch. The crisp, defined edge of satin stitching often makes it an ideal choice for man-made structures. Conversely, rough, gnarled edges could require a scribbling effect that can be accomplished with free-motion stitching. (Further information on both these techniques can be found on pages 39–43.)

People

Drawing people can be quite a challenge. If you do want to include people in silhouette form, just concentrate on the outline. If you are using your own photographs you have license to enlarge the image using a photocopier. It is then only a matter of tracing around the outline of the person, reversing the image to the back of your paper, and then tracing it on fusible web. Choose fabrics that are fairly dark but, if possible, have some subtle texture. Pure black fabrics tend to be quite stark.

Animals

Many travel brochures, especially those enticing us to visit Africa, feature fabulous photographs of wild animals in silhouette against a dramatic sky. For some people, sketching animals comes naturally, but for most of us our sketch of an elephant or giraffe looks more like a preschooler's drawing. To sketch an animal, use the plan of attack outlined above for people. You can enlarge your own images, but there are also some great resources available to assist you. Dover Publications has a range of books with copyright-free drawings of animals that are for personal use (see Resources, page 96).

Fisherman casts to collect bait.

Detail of figures from **Summer Sunset** by Lyn Johnstone (page 82)

Detail of elephant in **Ode to Westwood** by Jenny Collett (page 83)

Reflections

When you observe a still lake or river, the rocks, trees, banks, and other surrounding objects are reflected in the water as their mirror images. As the artist, you can decide whether you want to include these reflections in your composition.

Sometimes a reflection is so close to a perfect mirror image that knowing which is the right way up is difficult. In photos, a perfect reflection looks fine, but in a landscape painting or quilt, it will seem too perfect. Luckily, all it takes is a small amount of disturbance or breeze to make the reflection easier to paint or stitch.

Stunning reflections in gorge in northern Australia

Trees reflect as mirror images.

Use reflections to draw attention to the focal point of your composition. In this way, the reflections are not the main feature, but just a pleasing illusion that adds something extra to the design.

Factors that affect reflections include the roughness or movement of water; underwater objects such as rocks, sand, and weeds; and cloud and sky colors above. Paint reflections as simply as you can—just think of the shapes, colors, and tones.

The colors of reflections are similar to but less intense than the colors of the reflected objects. Just follow this easy rule—light reflects darker and dark reflects lighter. White objects reflected will appear grayer, and black objects will be lighter. Another general rule is that the reflection of the sky in clear water will look darker because it has lost some of its light.

A reflection is directly below the object being reflected. If the object is at an angle, the reflection is at the same angle, only reversed.

A reflection is usually the same height as the element being reflected. Measure the height of the object from its base and then repeat that distance from the base down toward the water. How much of the object will be reflected depends upon the distance of the object's base from the water. Disturbed water, however, plays tricks with reflections, scattering them so they are no longer the same height and width as the reflected objects.

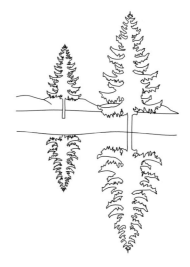

Amount of object reflected depends on distance of base from water.

When it comes to deciding on a technique to apply the reflection with, you can paint, stitch, or appliqué fabric. In most instances, I encourage my students to paint rather than apply fabric because you can vary the brushstrokes so the reflection is not too solid.

Detail of giraffe reflection in **Sunset Watering Hole** by Jenny Waddell (page 83)

To ensure that the reflection is a true mirror image, trace the outline of your original object onto the shiny side of freezer paper (this is the reverse side of what you normally draw on). Cut out the object and discard it. Iron the outside border of freezer paper in the correct place so it can act as a stencil. You can then relax as you apply paint to create an accurate and effective reflection. Alternatively, if you would prefer to stitch the reflection, you also have a great outline that you can fill in.

Apply paint to freezer-paper stencil.

An accurate and effective reflection

The darker tones of the reflected object can be broken up with horizontal lines of light to create the look of a horizontal water surface. To achieve this, brush on your paint with a horizontal movement, leaving small areas of the original water color visible. Alternatively, leave strips of the underneath fabric showing through as you stitch. Don't be tempted to quilt around the edge of a reflection. Quilt through as if the reflection doesn't exist. This will further enhance the notion that the water has a flat surface.

Shadows

Shadows can be important design elements in a landscape. They can connect areas and reveal the direction of the light. They can also be used to lead the viewer's eye to a particular section of the landscape.

Don't confuse shadows with reflections. Reflections will always be a near vertical mirror image of the reflected object, but the direction and length of the shadows will depend on the position of the source of light. There are no shadows when the sun is directly overhead, but as the sun sinks lower in the sky, shadows will gradually lengthen.

Don't make your shadows black, because black shadows tend to deaden your landscape. Cameras usually render shadows as black or almost black, with the reflected light that appears in real-life shadows completely lost. Try to make your shadows transparent, using some of the colors that you imagine would occur in the area, even though you don't really see them in your photograph. When searching for the right color for a shadow, try adding a small amount of the complement of the original color. Often shadows can be portrayed effectively in violet and blue tones with the under color shining through. Shadows are darker nearer the source, and their edges are often hazy and indistinct.

Borders

The borders of your quilt should complement the landscape and not distract the viewer from the main composition. To select your borders and bring out the best in your work, pin your landscape to your design wall and try various fabrics around the edges. Don't introduce any new colors; different shades and textures of the colors already in the quilt can be used for effective framing. Stand back and decide which one looks best.

Audition color combinations.

A frame that is a similar color will extend your work, with the landscape flowing visually out into the border. The framing becomes an extension of the work and emphasizes what is happening in the work. A contrasting border will make the work seem smaller by defining the edges of the work itself.

Audition a range of light and dark fabrics. Probably you will find that a dark border around a dark work will make the lighter areas stand out. Conversely, a light border around a light work will tend to emphasize the darker areas in the work. Occasionally, a border can confine a quilt too much, so leaves or other small images can be placed just into the border to break up the boundary and provide extra spark. A border that matches the color on one side of the quilt top and contrasts with the other sides can also be quite effective.

Water lily leaves spill out into border.

When making decisions about borders, you must also take into account where the quilt is to be hung, because wall color, position, size of space, and so on will also affect your choice of color and fabric. You may decide to forgo borders altogether and just add a binding.

Narrow Inner Borders

Picture framers often use a narrow border inside a large outer frame. The purpose of this inner border is to break up the movement of color flowing to the outer border. The inner border is especially useful for breaking up areas of dark color in the composition that link to a dark border fabric.

We can replicate this effect in fabric by making a ¼″ (7mm) or even an ⅛″ (3mm) inside border. There is a simple procedure you can follow to ensure that your narrow frame is symmetrical and the sides are parallel.

1. Prepare your quilt by removing as much tear-away stabilizer as possible without putting too much stress on your stitches, and then squaring up the quilt.

2. Cut the narrow border strips 1¼″ (3cm) wide by the needed length. Cutting the narrow borders wider than necessary gives you something to hold onto securely when sewing the borders and helps avoid stretching.

3. Pin and sew the borders in place as you would any other border. I always stitch the side borders first, and then the top and bottom, so that there are no distracting vertical lines heading out the top and bottom edges of the quilt. Be sure to press the seams toward the outer edge after stitching them.

4. Cut your outer border pieces to your desired width plus 1″ (2.5cm).

5. When you sew the outer borders to the quilt, pin and then sew the borders with the new border underneath the work. You want to be able to see the stitching line from the first, narrow border so that you can line up the left side of the ¼″ (7mm) presser foot with the previous stitching line. To create an even smaller border, line up the left inside edge of your presser foot with your initial stitching line, or alternatively, move your needle position to the left. The distance between your first stitching line and your second line of stitching will be the width of your inside border.

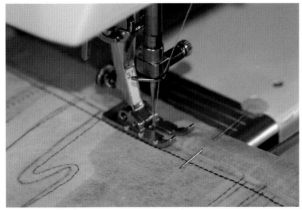

Line up edge of ¼″ (7mm) presser foot with first stitching line.

Narrow inner border gives extra definition.

6. Trim the seam allowances to ¼″ (7mm) and press them toward the outer border.

7. Attach the remaining borders in the same way.

Quilting

The quilting process will allow you to further enhance your design, but don't overdo the quilting. The quilting lines on a landscape need to add to the design and not cause a distraction. Your quilting lines must reflect the textures and contours of your landscape.

Layer the backing, batting, and quilt top using masking tape to anchor each of the three layers to a flat surface. Stretch each layer slightly so there are no creases or wrinkles. Baste the three layers together with safety pins approximately every 3–4″ (8–10cm).

Before you start quilting, read through the information presented on pages 47–49 on free-motion stitching.

Stitch in-the-ditch around the main elements using a matching thread as much as possible. This may be easier to do in invisible thread. Your next step is to add contour quilting following the direction of each element. As well as improving the perspective of your design, the quilting lines will give more texture to your surface. I try to match the color of my thread to the area I am working on unless I specifically need a contrast.

Look carefully at your original design to get help with the direction of your quilting lines. Some suggestions for quilting have been included in the illustrations below.

Sky

Use a minimum of quilting lines in the sky because the sky is light, and too much stitching gives a feeling of heaviness. Replicate the colors of the sky in your thread. Use a lighter thread because a darker quilting line will read like a dirty pencil mark in an illuminated sky. Just follow the patterns you have created in paint gently curving across the sky. The lines nearer the horizon should be closer together than those overhead.

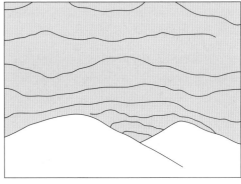

Use minimum of quilting lines in sky.

Mountains

Look carefully at the contours of the mountains and follow them with your quilting lines. Gentle hills are quilted in a different way than steep mountains. Cliffs need lots of vertical lines.

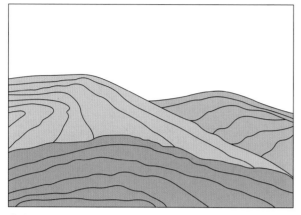

Quilt using contours of terrain as guide.

Water

When quilting a lake or large body of smooth water, keep your quilting lines fairly horizontal. Quilt right through reflections as if they don't exist. If the water is rough and turbulent, let your quilting lines echo the disturbances.

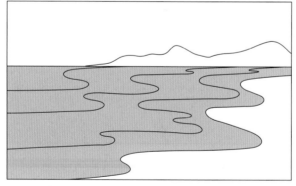

Keep quilting lines horizontal for calm water.

Flat Land

The lay of the land can be changed by the direction of your quilting lines. Try to suggest a ploughed field or vineyard. For flat areas, the lines will be mainly horizontal.

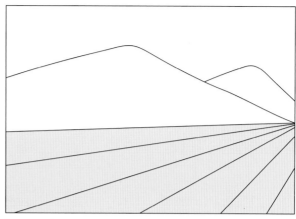

Direction of quilting lines defines lay of land.

Shorelines

Flowing contour lines in the sand can be effective, but once again, most of the lines are horizontal. Look at your photos and check the patterns left by the rhythm of the tides.

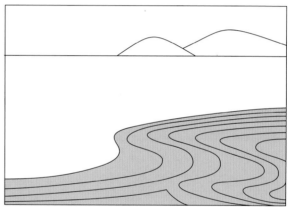

Contour lines show sand at low tide.

Rocks

Quilt around the outside edge of each rock and then outline cracks and crevices to help create perspective.

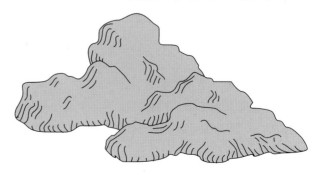

Stitch in cracks and crevices.

Trees

When you quilt your trees, use a matching colored thread around the trunks as close as possible to or even on the fused edge. This will help seal the edge to prevent further fraying. Quilt foliage, replicating the pattern of the foliage, adding enough stitching to give texture, but not so much that the canopy sinks into the quilt top.

Binding

Once again, the color choice is crucial when it comes to binding your quilt. Often the binding is the same color as the outside border so as not to introduce another distraction. For other landscapes, the binding is the only frame, and it needs to give some closure to the edge of the composition.

For most of my large quilts, I try to create a frame that harmonizes with the surrounding areas but still provides visual definition and support. I have found that I can do this successfully by adding a wide binding that has been specially dyed to match adjacent quilt areas. See the bindings on *Grass Trees* (page 15) and *Tidal Images* (page 24).

Quilts with borders and small quilts require a much narrower binding. Adjust the width of your strips accordingly.

Always square up the quilt sandwich because the edges may have become distorted slightly during the quilting. Cut the binding strips across the width of the fabric. Fold the strips in half lengthwise and press them.

Using a walking foot, sew the side binding strips first. Turn the folded edges to the back of the quilt and firmly hand stitch them in place. At the corners, trim the excess binding even with the edge of the quilt. Sew the top and bottom binding strips to the quilt, leaving a short overlap at each end. Turn the folded edges to the back of the quilt, tucking in the ends to give a neat, firm corner. Hand stitch the binding in place on the back.

Detail of *Tidal Images*
Binding is hand-dyed to create harmony and definition.

Cooktown Lighthouse, 28″ × 20″ (70cm × 50cm), Marilyn Hawkins

Summer Sunset, 18″ × 24″ (45cm × 60cm),
Lyn Johnstone

Sunset Over the Bay, 29″ × 33″ (74cm × 84cm),
Kathy Barber

The Banks of the Nambucca, 44″ × 34″ (110cm × 90 cm), Kathy Barber

Eerie Glow, 31$\frac{1}{2}$″ × 24$\frac{1}{4}$″ (80cm × 62cm), Patricia Daly

Ode to Westwood, 42″ × 45″ (107cm × 114cm), Jenny Collett

Sunset Watering Hole, 16$\frac{1}{2}$″ × 24$\frac{1}{2}$″ (41cm × 61cm), Jenny Waddell

Outback, 27″ × 20″ (70cm × 50cm), Jeannie Henry

African Thorn Tree

African Thorn Tree, 16½″ × 12″ (42cm × 30.5cm), Gloria Loughman

Original photo that provided the theme for this project

After teaching at the Celebrations quilt festival in Durban, South Africa, in 2004, we visited the Hluhluwe Game Reserve, where we were able to observe and photograph amazing wildlife, spectacular scenery, and magnificent trees. One of the most fascinating was the umbrella thorn tree, the quintessential African tree. These trees provide both food and shelter for the animals that live on the grasslands.

Fabric Requirements

Sky: ¼ yard or an 8″ × 17″ (20cm × 43cm) piece of hand-painted cotton or a commercial sky fabric

Hill: ⅛ yard or a 3″ × 17″ (8cm × 43cm) piece of rusty orange fabric

Background tree line and clumps of trees: ⅛ yard or a 3″ × 17″ (8cm × 43cm) piece of dark brown fabric

Foreground land: ¼ yard or a 5″ × 17″ (13cm × 43cm) piece of olive green fabric

Foreground water: ¼ yard or a 5″ × 17″ (13cm × 43cm) piece of dark gold fabric (similar to sky color but darker)

Thorn tree trunk: ⅓ yard or a 9″ × 13″ (23cm × 33cm) piece of charcoal black fabric

Thorn tree foliage: ¼ yard or a 5″ × 14″ (13cm × 36cm) piece of variegated brown and olive green fabric

Narrow border: ⅛ yard or a 4″ × 40″ (10cm × 100cm) piece of gold fabric

Backing: ½ yard or a 20″ × 15″ (50cm × 38cm) piece of fabric

Wide binding: ⅜ yard or an 11″ × 40″ (28cm × 100cm) piece of brown fabric

Other Supplies

Freezer paper

Tear-away stabilizer: ½ yard (50cm) of 40″ (1m)-wide tear-away stabilizer or similar fabric stabilizer

Fusible web: 1 yard (1m) of WonderUnder (17″/43cm wide) or ½ yard (50cm) of Vliesofix (36″/90cm wide) fusible web, or a similar product

Batting: 20″ × 15″ (50cm × 38cm)

Thread to match fabrics

Construction

The project pattern is on the pullout at the back of the book.

Refer to the fused landscape method of construction on pages 57–59 for detailed instructions.

Background

1. Trace the pattern onto tear-away stabilizer.

2. Trace the outlines of the sky piece onto the paper side of freezer paper (not the shiny side). Iron the freezer paper onto the right side of the sky fabric. Cut out the sky piece with ½″ (1.3cm) seam allowances and pin it into position on the tear-away stabilizer.

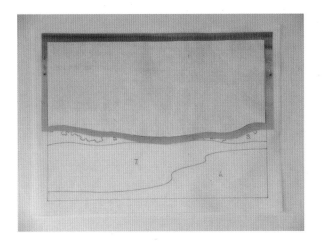

3. Transfer the lines to the reverse side of the pattern to avoid getting a mirror image. Trace the landscape pieces onto fusible web, extending the edges of the trees, hill, and water to create ¼″ (7mm) seam allowances to tuck under adjacent pieces.

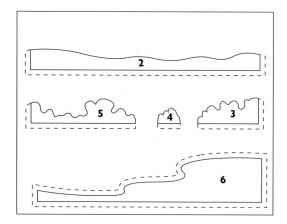

4. Iron the pieces of fusible web onto the backs of the selected fabrics. Cut out the pieces on the dashed and solid lines.

5. Fuse the pieces in order to the tear-away stabilizer. Piece 7 is added last.

6. Use matching thread to straight stitch along the edges of the pieces.

7. Remove the tear-away stabilizer behind the sky piece. The rest of the stabilizer can be left in position.

Quilting

1. Trim the sides of your quilt top to 15″ × 10½″ (38cm × 27cm), making sure that the corners are square.
2. Cut the backing fabric and batting to 20″ × 15″ (50cm × 38cm).
3. Sandwich your quilt, pinning the 3 layers together with safety pins.
4. Stitch in-the-ditch along the edge of the fused shapes using matching thread.
5. Add some quilting lines to the land, water, and sky pieces.

Borders

1. Cut 2 strips 1¼″ (3cm) by the width of the fabric for the narrow inner borders.
2. Add the borders (see directions on pages 78–79).

Trunk

1. Transfer the lines of the trunk to the reverse side of the pattern to avoid getting a mirror image. Trace the trunk pattern onto fusible web.
2. Iron the fusible web onto the back of the selected fabric. Cut out the piece on the lines.

3. Fuse the trunk in place. Use matching thread to free-motion stitch the trunk.

Fuse trunk in position and free-motion stitch.

Binding

1. Cut 2 strips 4½″ (11cm) wide by the width of the fabric. Fold the strips in half lengthwise and press them.

2. Trim the excess backing and batting even with the edge of the narrow border. The inside border should now measure 1″ (2.5cm).

3. Pin the side binding pieces in position with the raw edges ⅝″ (1.6cm) from the outside edge of the quilt. Use a gridded ruler as a guide.

4. Turn your quilt to the back and stitch ⅛″ (3mm) on the outside of the border stitching line. Use the ⅛″ (3mm) mark on your ¼″ foot or simply adjust your needle position to give you the correct measurement. (Refer to pages 78–79 for detailed information on this technique.)

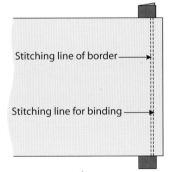

Stitching line of border

Stitching line for binding

Sew from back ⅛″ (3mm) on outside of initial stitching line.

5. Finish attaching the binding (refer to page 81). Pin and sew the top and bottom binding pieces in the same way.

(Refer to pages 78–79 for detailed information on this technique.)

TIP

Use a gridded ruler to make sure that your borders are perfectly placed.

Foliage and Reeds

1. Fuse the foliage in place and then free-motion zigzag around the edges and sky holes, stitching off the foliage onto the sky piece to give a rough, prickly edge.

2. Use the pattern as a guide to free-motion stitch some reeds and grass using an appropriate colored thread. A variegated thread works well to give the illusion of different shades of vegetation.

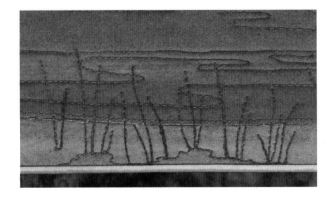

Tropical Escape

Tropical Escape, 20$\frac{1}{2}$″ × 17$\frac{1}{2}$″ (52cm × 44cm), Gloria Loughman

Many people dream of relaxing on a warm, tropical beach, gazing at a beautiful sunset over the water. Paint your own magical sunset and then build up this landscape using some of the techniques covered earlier in this book.

Fabric Requirements

Sky: ⅓ yard or a 10″ × 16″ (25cm × 41cm) piece of hand-painted cotton or a commercial sky fabric

Sea: ⅛ yard or a 3″ × 16″ (8cm × 41cm) piece each of 6 fabrics ranging from deep red-violet to pale pink-violet

Sea highlight: ⅛ yard or a 3″ × 16″ (8cm × 41cm) piece of pale orange-pink fabric

Foreground land: ⅛ yard or a 3″ × 16″ (8cm × 41cm) piece of fabric that is dark but lighter than the tree trunk fabric

Palm tree trunks: ⅓ yard or an 11″ × 16″ (28cm × 41cm) piece of dark violet fabric

Palm fronds: ¼ yard or an 8″ × 18″ (20cm × 46cm) piece each of a dark violet fabric and a lighter mauve variegated fabric

Narrow border: ⅛ yard or a 4″ × 40″ (10cm × 100cm) piece of gold fabric

Outer border: ⅜ yard or a 12″ × 40″ (30cm × 100cm) piece of dark violet fabric

Backing: ⅔ yard or a 23″ × 20″ (58cm × 50cm) piece of fabric

Binding: ⅓ yard or a 10″ × 40″ (25cm × 100cm) piece of dark violet fabric

Other Supplies

Freezer paper

Tear-away stabilizer: ½ yard (50cm) of 40″ (1m)-wide tear-away stabilizer or similar fabric stabilizer

Fusible web: 1 yard (1m) of WonderUnder (17″/43cm wide) or ½ yard (50cm) of Vliesofix (36″/90cm wide) fusible web, or a similar product

Batting: 23″ × 20″ (58cm × 50cm)

Invisible thread

Thread to match fabrics

Construction

The project pattern is on the pullout at the back of the book.

Refer to the contoured landscape method of construction on pages 51–54 for detailed instructions.

Background

1. Trace the pattern onto tear-away stabilizer.
2. Trace the outlines of pieces (2–11) onto the paper side of the freezer paper (not the shiny side). Include the numbers and arrows. Cut out these pieces on the lines.
3. Iron the freezer-paper patterns onto the right sides of the selected fabrics. Use the same fabric for pieces 3 and 5. Use the highlight fabric for pieces 7 and 9.

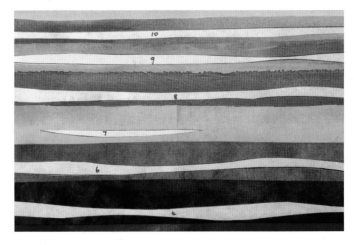

4. Cut out the pieces with ½″ (1.3cm) seam allowances. Trim the lower edges of pieces 3–10 and the upper edge of piece 11 to ¼″ (7mm). These edges are marked with arrows.

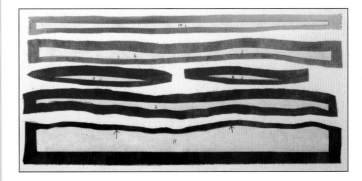

5. Press the ¼″ (7mm) seam allowance to the back on pieces 3–11.

6. Position piece 2, with the freezer paper still attached, on the stabilizer. Use the traced pattern on the stabilizer as your guide for correct placement. Pin the piece in position.

7. Place piece 3 in position and pin it at right angles every 2″ (5cm). Repeat this process with pieces 4–10, removing the freezer paper when the adjacent piece is in place.

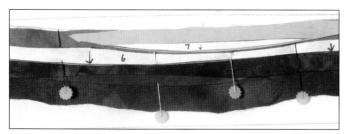

8. Stitch the pieces using invisible appliqué (see pages 45–46).

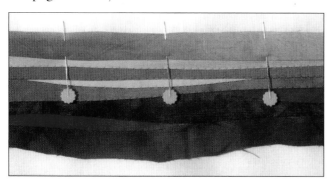

9. Place the sky and the stitched water pieces right sides together. Line up the horizon edge of the sky with the top edge of piece 10 and pin the pieces in place. Sew across the horizon edge of the sky from the back of the stabilizer, using the drawn horizon line as your stitching guide. Turn the work back to the right side. Flip the sky piece up and pin it in position.

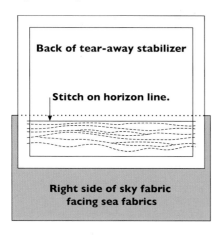

10. Pin the foreground piece (piece 11) into position, remove the freezer paper, and stitch.

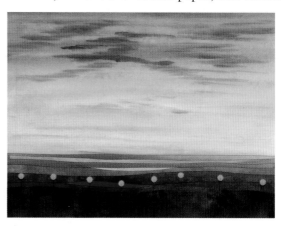

Palm Trees

1. Transfer the lines to the reverse side of the pattern to avoid getting a mirror image. Trace the trunk and frond patterns onto fusible web.

2. Iron the fusible web onto the back of the selected fabrics. Cut the pieces on the lines. Use small scissors to cut out the fronds.

3. Fuse the trunks and fronds in place.

4. Use matching thread to free-motion stitch the pieces. Stitch off the edges of each frond onto the background to create a feathering effect. (Refer to technique 4 on page 69 for a detailed description of the techniques used to create the fine textures of the palm trees.)

5. Use variegated threads to build up a range of colors in the foliage.

6. Use free-motion stitching to create grass around the base of the trees.
7. Gently remove as much of the tear-away stabilizer as possible without putting too much pressure on the stitches.

Borders

1. Trim the edges of the quilt top, making sure the corners are square.
2. Cut 2 strips 1¼″ (3cm) wide by the width of the fabric for the narrow inner borders. Cut 3 strips 3½″ (9cm) wide by the width of the fabric for the outer borders.
3. Add the borders, making the inner borders ¼″ (7mm) wide. (Directions are on pages 78–79).

Quilting

1. Cut the backing fabric and batting to 23″ × 20″ (58cm × 50cm).
2. Sandwich your quilt, pinning the 3 layers together with safety pins.
3. Stitch along the edges of the small border. Quilt around the palm tree trunks using a matching thread. Free-motion quilt the foliage, repeating the shape of the embroidery stitching but to a much lesser extent.
4. Stitch in-the-ditch along some of the lines in the sea and the foreground. Add some quilting lines to the sky piece.

Binding

1. Cut 3 strips 2½″ (6.5cm) wide by the width of the fabric. Fold the strips in half lengthwise and press them.
2. Trim the excess batting and backing.
3. Pin the side binding pieces in position, lining up the raw edges with the edges of the quilt.
4. Attach the binding pieces with ⅜″ (1cm) seams.
5. Finish attaching the binding (refer to page 81). Pin and sew the top and bottom binding pieces in the same way.

Mohave Yuccas

Original photo that provided the theme for this project

Mojave Yuccas, 15⅞″ × 21½″ (40.5cm × 52cm), Gloria Loughman

In 2005, after teaching a class in Palm Springs, California, we spent a fabulous day visiting Joshua Tree National Park. As well as photographing the remarkable Joshua trees, we came across a family of yuccas gathered together to create an imposing silhouette.

Fabric Requirements

Sky: ¼ yard or a 6″ × 40″ (15cm × 100cm) piece each of 6 to 8 fabrics that blend well together. Include some light- and medium-tone fabrics to create contrast.

Back hill: ⅛ yard or a 3″ × 13″ (8cm × 33cm) piece of rusty brown fabric

Front hill: ⅛ yard or a 3″ × 17″ (8cm × 43cm) piece of deeper brown fabric

Foreground land: ¼ yard or an 8″ × 17″ (20cm × 43cm) piece of rust textured fabric

Yuccas: ½ yard or a 16″ × 40″ (40cm × 100cm) piece of dark green fabric

Backing: ¾ yard or a 19″ × 25″ (48cm × 64cm) piece of fabric

Binding: ⅜ yard or a 12″ × 40″ (30cm × 100cm) piece of black fabric

Other Supplies

Freezer paper

Tear-away stabilizer: ⅔ yard (60cm) of 40″ (1m)-wide tear-away stabilizer or similar fabric stabilizer

Fusible web: 1 yard (1m) of WonderUnder (17″/43cm wide) or ½ yard (50cm) of Vliesofix (36″/90cm wide) fusible web, or a similar product

Batting: 19″ × 25″ (48cm × 64cm)

Invisible thread

Thread to match fabrics

Construction

The project pattern is on the pullout at the back of the book.

Refer to the mosaic landscape method of construction on pages 54–57 for detailed instructions.

Background

1. Trace the pattern onto tear-away stabilizer.

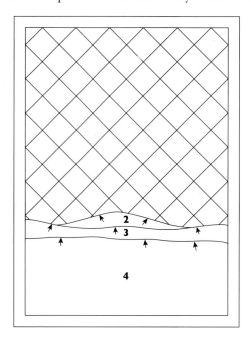

2. Trace the outlines of the hills and foreground pieces onto the freezer paper, shiny side down. Include the numbers and arrows. Cut out these pieces on the lines.
3. Cut 85 squares 2¼″ × 2¼″ (5.7cm × 5.7cm) from the sky fabrics. Cut approximately 10 squares from each fabric to get started. Arrange the squares on the tear-away stabilizer, overlapping the marked lines.

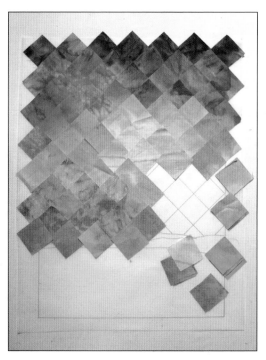

4. Try to get a smooth flow of color across the squares without distracting color jumps. It will be necessary to cut extra squares of some fabrics. When you are happy with the arrangement, sew the squares together in diagonal rows.

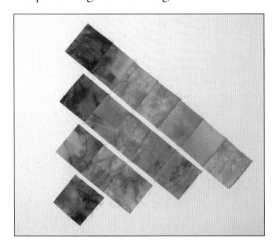

5. Press the seam allowances for each row in opposite directions so that you can butt the seams for accurate piecing. Pin across each opposing seam allowance and sew the rows together with an accurate ¼″ (7mm) seam.

6. Press the joined rows, pressing the seam allowances in one direction.

7. Pin the pieced sky area in place on the stabilizer.

8. Iron the freezer-paper patterns for the hills and foreground pieces (2–4) onto the right sides of the selected fabrics. Cut the pieces with ½″ (1.3cm) seam allowances. Trim the top edges of the pieces to ¼″ (7mm). These edges are marked with arrows.

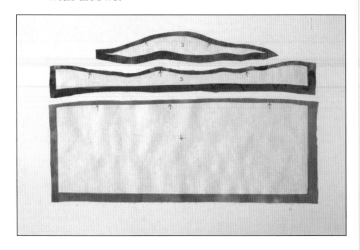

9. Press the ¼″ (7mm) seam allowances to the back on the pieces.

10. Position piece 2, with the freezer paper still attached, on the stabilizer. Use the traced pattern on the stabilizer as your guide for correct placement. Pin the piece in position.

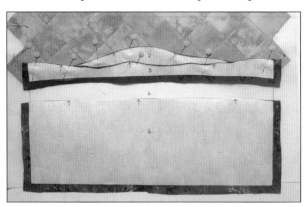

11. Repeat this process with pieces 3 and 4. Pin the pieces at right angles every 2″ (5cm). Remove the freezer paper when the adjacent piece is in place.

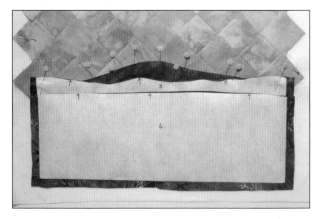

12. Stitch the pieces using invisible appliqué (described on pages 45–46).

Yuccas

1. Transfer the lines to the reverse side of the pattern to avoid getting a mirror image. Trace the trunk and spiky head shapes separately onto fusible web, and cut out leaving ¼″ (7mm) around the outside of the lines.

2. Iron the fusible web onto the back of the selected fabric. Cut the pieces on the lines.

3. Fuse the trunks and head shapes in place. Use matching thread to free-motion stitch the pieces. You can use your darning foot to free-motion stitch each shape, or alternatively, carefully work your way around each edge with a straight stitch using a foot that gives you a clear view.

4. Gently remove as much of the tear-away stabilizer as possible without putting too much pressure on the stitches.

Quilting

1. Cut backing fabric and batting to 19″ × 25″ (48cm × 64cm).

2. Sandwich your quilt, pinning the 3 layers together with safety pins.

3. Quilt around each yucca. Add some quilting lines to the sky, hill, and foreground pieces.

Binding

1. Cut 3 strips 3″ (7.5cm) wide by the width of the fabric. Fold the strips in half lengthwise and press them.

2. Measure ½″ (1.3cm) outside the center of the squares on the side edges of the sky area. Trim the side of the hill and foreground areas even with this line. Do not trim the squares on the edges at this stage. Trim the bottom edge, making sure the corners are square.

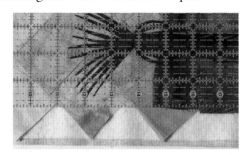

3. Pin the side binding strips in position, lining up the raw edges ½″ (1.3cm) outside the center of the squares.

4. Sew the side binding strips with ½″ (1.3cm) seam allowances.

5. Finish attaching the binding (refer to page 81). Pin and sew the top and bottom binding strips in the same way.

Alternative Ideas

A number of different shapes could be highlighted against this type of background. Cacti or other strong, identifiable shapes could be featured as silhouettes.

Cacti provide inspiration for wonderful silhouettes.

About the Author

Gloria Loughman lives in Kerang, a small Australian town famous for its duck shooting and ibis rookery. She is married and has three daughters. Gloria trained as a secondary school teacher and worked mainly in literacy and special education faculties. Her initiation into the world of patchwork occurred approximately sixteen years ago, when she was recovering from a rugged course of chemotherapy.

Over the years she has dabbled in many areas, including strip piecing, bargello, colorwash, fabric dyeing and painting, and machine embroidery. After completing studies in design and color as part of a Diploma of Art in 1996, she began to make her large vivid landscape quilts depicting the Australian bush. These quilts have won many major awards in Australia, Europe, Japan, and the United States. Her quilt *Kimberley Mystique* was the winner of Australia's most prestigious national quilting award in 2003.

Gloria loves sharing her knowledge and skills with others. She likes to challenge her students to design their own landscape quilts but is also happy to provide patterns. Many students come back for a second or third class.

As well as being in demand as a teacher, Gloria has curated six exhibitions of Australian quilts in the United States, and has had the privilege of judging at many major shows. Her work has been featured in many books and magazines.

What began as a therapy has developed into a passion and has given Gloria the opportunity to travel the world exhibiting her quilts, teaching classes, and meeting lots of wonderful people.

Resources

FABRIC PAINT

HI STRIKE FABRIC PAINT
Batik Oetoro
203 Avoca St.
Randwick, NSW 2031
Australia
www.dyeman.com

SETACOLOR FABRIC PAINT
Pro Chemical and Dye
P.O. Box 14
Somerset, MA 02726
USA
800-228-9393
www.prochemical.com

DHARMA TRADING CO.
P.O. Box 150916
San Rafael, CA 94915
USA
800-542-5227
www.dharmatrading.com

HAND PAINTED FABRIC

SKYDYES, MICKEY LAWLER
P.O. Box 370116
West Hartford, CT 06137-0116
USA
www.skydyes.com

THREAD

SUPERIOR THREADS
P.O. Box 1672
St. George, UT 84771
USA
www.superiorthreads.com

COPYRIGHT-FREE IMAGES

DOVER PUBLICATIONS
www.doverpublications.com

QUILTING SUPPLIES

COTTON PATCH MAIL ORDER
3405 Hall Lane, Dept. CTB
Lafayette, CA 94595
USA
800-835-4418
925-283-7883
email: quiltusa@yahoo.com
website: www.quiltusa.com
Note: Fabrics used in the quilts shown may not be currently available since fabric manufacturers keep most fabrics in print for only a short time.

FOR MORE INFORMATION, WRITE FOR A FREE CATALOG:

C&T Publishing, Inc.
P.O. Box 1456
Lafayette, CA 94549
USA
800-284-1114
email: ctinfo@ctpub.com
website: www.ctpub.com